Life Choices:
Pursuing Your Passion

What Others Are Saying About This Book

This wonderful book can help you find your passion. Written with wisdom and guidance, it is more than just another inspirational book.
—Tom Antion, Founder
The Internet Marketing Training Center of Virginia, www.IMTCVA.org

As I've grown older, I know in my heart the simple importance of finding a bit of thoughtful inspiration each day. This book is a timely reminder that it's all about what we choose. We are not the victim of events beyond our control, but rather the master of our choices.
—Jeff Dewar, CEO, *Quality Digest Magazine*

This book gives real life examples of how to move beyond fear and frustration and make every minute count.
—Dr. Casey McNeal, Author
Building Relationships: Effective Strategies For How to Work With People

There is wisdom in every word, depth on every page – written by the heart.
—Tom Cottrell, Author, *Runners Guide*

So many people talk about achieving work-life balance, but few know where to start. The authors and stories collected in this book demonstrate how to achieve those goals and build a lifestyle that perfectly marries our need to work with our desire to live life to its fullest. Read on fearless voyager!
—Paul H. Burton, Creator of the QuietSpacing® Productivity Method

The authors messages of personal empowerment show you how to stop making excuses and pursue your passion in order to venture out of your comfort zone and achieve the success you desire.
—Rollan A. Roberts II
Author of international best-sellers
Riot: An Assault on Modern Leadership, Born to Dream, & Born to Be Rich

Life Choices

Pursuing Your Passion

Jeff Civillico

Dallas Humble

Justina Rudez

Mary Monaghan

Darren LaCroix

Ridgely Goldsborough

Charlyn Shelton

Anthony Spinicchia

Charlotte Foust

Jan Mills

Cindi R. Maciolek

Jenna Doughton

Sandy Kastel

Bill Lynch

Kevin B. Parsons

Judi Moreo

Dolores Ramsey McLaughlin

Marisa Wollheim

April Aimee Adams

Ann Parenti

Bea Goodwin

Cheryl Smith

Laura Peters

Sandra Gore Nielsen

Anne Dreyer

Ginette Osier Bedsaul

Turning Point

INTERNATIONAL

LAS VEGAS, NEVADA

Editor: Jami Carpenter
Cover design and typesetting: Ambush Graphics

Library of Congress Control Number: 2011921432
ISBN: 978-0-9825264-3-9

INTERNATIONAL

Post Office Box 231360
Las Vegas, Nevada 89105

www.lifechoicesbook.com

Published in the United States of America

Dedication

In memory of

Dottie Walters

who inspired so many of us to pursue our passions
and
achieve our dreams.

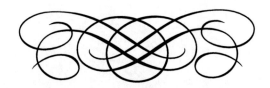

To live is to choose. But to choose well, you must know who you are and what you stand for, where you want to go and why you want to get there.

—Kofi Annan
Seventh Secretary-General
of the United Nations

Contents

$\mathcal{P}$ersistence

There is no passion to be found playing small - in settling for a life that is less than the one you are capable of living.

—*Nelson Mandela*

j

a

in

it c

that

1

sible v

writter

of poss

Do What You Love;
Love What You Do

JEFF CIVILLICO

Four years after college graduation, I returned to my Georgetown University homecoming to find that most of my friends were seemingly unsatisfied in their professional lives. How could it be that so many intelligent and motivated young professionals were finding fulfillment elusive in the "real" world? Keep in mind—we're talking about graduates of the top business and law schools across the country.

Surprisingly, my career as a performer was all the buzz. "You're so LUCKY to be able to do what you love for a living."

I juggle plungers. And I'm the lucky one.

Further conversation revealed that although everyone agreed it was theoretically possible to create an enterprise based on passion, the undertaking seemed unrealistic and impractical to most. How are you going to pay the bills? How do you meet the right people to help you? What if you don't have some weird talent like juggling?

Clearly there existed a gap between understanding the importance of a career based on passion and understanding how to brand, market, and monetize that passion.

Today, the professional paradigm for most people bears little resemblance to the experience of previous generations. Platforms of business have changed. Traditional industries have soured. A typical employee might look more like an independent contractor, and the social media revolution has completely altered the way we communicate. In this climate of extreme change, there lives unparalleled access and opportunity.

Realistically, if one sat down to choose a career based solely on personal and financial fulfillment, we can all agree that juggling probably would not make the top-ten list. Yet I have been able to brand my passion for juggling in a way that affords me a very comfortable and deeply gratifying lifestyle...not to mention a ridiculously fun one.

What do you think of when you hear the word "juggler?" Clowns? The circus? A birthday party? You probably don't think of sailing on the Queen Mary II, bungee jumping in New Zealand, sky diving in Australia, getting inside the White House, the Kennedy Center, the Ronald Reagan building, visiting the Taj Mahal, Europe, and Malaysia.

Juggling has afforded me all of these opportunities—either directly or indirectly. How is this possible? I discovered my core competency, I packaged my services, and I positioned them in a way that was attractive to the marketplace. Remember—I juggle plungers.

After analyzing the branding of my juggling, I came up with seven pillars—Seven *"Ps" of Success*—that I believe can help anyone create the career, and lifestyle, of their dreams: Passion, Philosophy, Personal Brand, Power Team, Plan, Proactivity, and Performance.

Please note:

This is not a linear, systematic road map of bullet points but rather a discussion of interconnected ideas. I don't think it is possible to create a step-by-step handbook for taking a hobby and branding it. "Branding your passion" is an art, and therefore needs to happen organically. When you understand the larger concepts at play, the daily to-do lists will take care of themselves.

When I talk about "branding your passion," I'm speaking not only about being an entrepreneur, but also being an "intra-preneur." You can just as easily brand your passion in your role within your company, within your school, or within your family.

1) Passion

Passion is the fuel that drives any endeavor.

Are you passionate? Notice I didn't ask, "What's your passion?" I believe that's the wrong question. That elicits a response like—"I don't have any weird talent like juggling. I can't sing, I don't play sports—I don't have any passions."

This is backwards. I believe it's the rare case when someone drifts through life, suddenly finds something that moves him, and then instantly transforms into a different kind of person—one who cares, who has an intense drive and a desire to make things happen. Can this life-transformation occur? Sure. But generally speaking, that's a remarkably one-sided view. More often, passionate people wake up every day with an intense desire to become more than they were the day before—mentally, physically, spiritually, and socially. They connect with projects they believe in, and channel their passion through that endeavor. The energy flows in both directions.

In his bestselling book, *Linchpin* (1992), Seth Godin writes: "Passion isn't project-specific. It's people-specific. Some people are hooked on passion, deriving their sense of self from the act of being passionate. Perhaps your challenge isn't finding a better project...Perhaps you need to get in touch with what it means to feel passionate. People with passion look for ways to make things happen."

As a kid, I went from one hobby to the next—completely engrossing myself in whatever it was at the time. My parents talked of "Jeff's obsessions." I collected rocks, I collected stamps ... looking back at the other options, I think I actually became the least nerdy kid possible by choosing juggling. WOW.

My passion has changed over the years. At first it was hardcore, technical juggling. I wanted to juggle more stuff than the other guy, and win more medals at the world juggling competitions (yes, there are world juggling competitions!)

Then my passion became entertaining. I quickly learned that the audience didn't care about juggling—they wanted to laugh, to connect—they wanted to be entertained. I loved the feeling of making an audience laugh. What a rush! My quest became to craft interactive juggling routines in a way that built a strong rapport with my audience.

Today, my passion is connecting with people—on stage and off. I've learned what really thrills me is bringing people together, whether it's laughing together with a huge crowd for forty-five minutes on stage at a corporate event, talking to one person after a show for five minutes, or building my non-profit, Win-Win Entertainment, to match willing performers with charity events in need.

The point is I am not hooked on juggling. I am hooked on passion.

~ *Don't complain that you don't have anything to be passionate about. Work on becoming a passionate person, and you will have plenty to be passionate about.* ~

2) Philosophy

Your philosophy is your set of values that underlies everything you do. You may think that a life philosophy is some grandiose notion that doesn't apply to you—you don't have one, and you don't need one. Yet you *do* have a philosophy, whether you know it or not. Your work ethic, your goals, your direction—all of these contribute to who you are and your philosophy. If you don't think about any of these ideas and you don't want to, that's a philosophy too.

There will be times when your philosophy is challenged. Perhaps it's the opportunity to take a shortcut by acting less than moral. Perhaps it's stabbing someone in the back who helped you get where you are.

Make your philosophy your policy. For some reason, people don't mess with policy. Think about stores: No returns—that's the policy. When your philosophy becomes your policy that means you abide by it all the time, no matter what. It's not even up for debate, which makes temptation less likely to creep in.

~ *Develop your philosophy and stick to it. It will be tested when you are not expecting it. Write it out and make it your policy. 100 percent is easier to maintain than 99 percent.* ~

3) Personal Brand

Your personal brand is an outer manifestation of your inner philosophy. It's how the world identifies and categorizes you from the actions you take.

Personal brand is about trust. Think of why you choose a brand-name product over a generic. When you buy the brand, you are buying into that product as something that has been tested and is reliable.

Are you on time? Do you carry yourself well? Are you articulate? Do you smile? Are you a good listener? Do you make eye contact? Do you follow through on what you say you're going to do? As an entertainer, I always think of this: When the lights go down, do you deliver… whether or not you've had a bad day, you feel sick, you're nervous, etc? Do you deliver? All of these things create your personal brand.

Today, your personal brand and professional brand are inextricably linked. Social media and the internet have blurred the line between who you are at home and who you are at work. No more double lives. Everything is out in the open now.

With more outsourcing happening all the time, your humanity is the difference. It's what makes you *you*, and ideally it's what makes you indispensable.

~ The more you can put into your job, the more humanized it becomes, the more irreplaceable you become. Work on minimizing the difference between your personal and professional brand. ~

4) Power Team

If you think about the number of people you come in contact with throughout a day, it's mind-blowing…especially if you're out doing your thing. The more you work, the more people in your field you connect with, the more your network grows exponentially. The trick is getting those people to "stick."

Imagine if every one of the people you come in contact with in your life markets you…for free! The woman next to you on the airplane who asks what you do for a living, the family you met on a cruise last year, etc. I'm not suggesting they're going to be making calls on your behalf, but rather engaging in a more subtle form of marketing. Think of someone you regard highly on a personal and professional level. When a topic arises related to that person, you jump right in and speak well of him or her. "Oh, you know so-and-so; isn't she a great girl? So talented, too. If you haven't seen her …" Imagine if everyone were talking about *you*.

With the internet and social media, opportunities to spread a good word are limitless—status updates, embedding YouTube clips in your blog, tweets, etc.

I have a friend who is always negative. I'll casually mention that I met a nice person after my show and he instantly wants to know what that guy can *do* for me. I don't know and I don't care. I naturally enjoy connecting with new people. This "one-for-one" thinking is unproductive and obsolete.

Business is about relationships. Relationships take time to build, and a certain amount of good fortune with timing. Who knows what could happen down the line? But really…who cares? Connect with people in the present moment.

~ Become a connector. Don't worry about one-for-one relationship payoffs. ~

5) Plan

Being self-employed grants you tremendous freedom. I can't tell you how many times I've gone for a four-hour bike ride on a weekday morning. I'm taking a couple of weeks off later this year to climb Mt. Kilimanjaro with some friends. I can work whenever I want—*if* I plan accordingly.

Outsiders looking in rarely see the other side: with freedom comes tremendous responsibility. Nobody is paying me, and at the end of the day, nobody is looking out for me *except* me. I need to continuously plan my life, and in that sense, I am always working. Whereas others leave their jobs and are finished for the day, I eat, sleep, and breathe entertainment. Even if I'm watching a game, I'm usually on my laptop at the same time. In terms of number of hours, I work longer than most of my peers. The catch, of course, is that I rarely view what I'm doing as "work," so for me it's a net win.

In addition to planning your present life's work, you also need to plan for a bigger operation than you currently have. It's part of the old "act as if" personal development mentality. When you "act as if" something already is a certain way, you carry yourself with a confidence that tends to create a self-fulfilling situation. When you build a system that can handle a dramatically increased workload, you are prepared. You are ready and, when you need to, can outsource all of the logistics which are not part of your core competency. You can outsource everything that doesn't make you *you*.

Planning is a continual practice of looking backward and forward. The often-overlooked part of planning is reflection. Some people are so stuck in their ways that they never actually stop to see if what they're doing is working. You should be constantly tweaking your plans, updating your system, looking back on what has worked and what has not in order to build an even more successful future.

~ Plan, reflect, and develop your system for success on a regular basis. The more efficient your system, the better you are. ~

6) Proactive

Everybody looks out for #1. It's not selfish. It's natural, and there's nothing wrong with it—it's our default setting. People are well-intentioned in their desire to help one another, but life sometimes gets in the way—*their* life. Their script goes something like this. "Sure, I said I'd recommend someone I just worked with, and I really would like to, but when I get home I've got family commitments, plans with friends, and business issues to address…not to mention ninety-seven new emails and four new voicemails. My default setting kicks back in, and I just never get around to making that call for a friend."

The solution? Be proactive! Take the initiative. In this case—follow up!

When you're on the fence about whether or not to be proactive and send that reminder email, drop by an office to introduce yourself, or bring up a necessary but maybe awkward issue, always choose *yes*. Make it your policy.

Will there be times when being proactive will cause you rejection? Absolutely. You may come off as being "too much," "too forward," "too aggressive." Are you going to allow a concern over how you might be perceived by a few to hold you back? Even if you're met with resistance, on some level, you will be regarded with respect for your willingness to ask for what you want, to put yourself out there, and to face potential rejection.

Some may disagree, but I believe that you have to risk occasionally irritating others by being too proactive. The cost of choosing *no*, quietly moving along, and always playing it safe is just too high.

~ *When you're debating whether or not to be proactive in a situation that may take you out of your comfort zone, force yourself always to say* **yes**. *Be proactive. Proactivity initiates forward momentum which leads to performance.* ~

7) Performance

Here's the fastest, easiest way to stand out among your peers:

Say you're going to do something. Do it. Repeat.

That's it. If that seems easy, it is. A good friend of mine always says, "It's easy to be a superstar because so few people are trying."

Let's take this seemingly trivial example: You say you will email a friend pictures after an event. You get home, and you email the pictures. Your friend is blown away by how quickly you did the task. (How long did it take—forty-five seconds?) Most people don't actually *do* what they say they will do and do it promptly.

Make yourself remember—write it down, make a digital note on your phone, email yourself a reminder—whatever works for you and your system. Just email the pictures!

Being busy is no longer an excuse. Everyone is busy, or at least thinks they are. Citing "busy" as a reason for lack of accomplishment of a certain task is almost a putdown to the party at the other end. You're implying that they're not as busy, i.e., successful, as you are.

I operate all facets of my life at an extremely fast pace. I am most comfortable when I take action quickly and adjust as I move forward. I feel like a cruise ship or an airplane with a target on the radar, constantly correcting my direction as I go along.

That's my system; that's my brand.

I have acquired a very good reputation for doing things. People come to me when they want something done. When they email me, they know they will get a fast response with action taken. This is a key part of my brand today.

~ Develop and live up to a reputation for consistent prompt action. Over time, this will put you in the top 10 percent of your industry. ~

Conclusion

Work harder on yourself than you do on your job.

~ Jim Rohn

These seven principles boil down to one simple idea: The key is not to spend time working specifically on these principles, but rather to spend time becoming the type of person who would naturally live these principles. It's a small but essential difference.

I believe self-help books often fail to connect with their audience because they focus on XYZ steps for success. A list of linear to-do steps seems calculated, forced, and unrealistic. "You can't teach that!" They make it seem easier than it is because that's what will sell. People don't want to hear that they have to change who they are at their core.

I fully acknowledge the goal here is to become the type of person who doesn't need to analyze how these principles operate in one's daily life, but focusing on these principles first will work if the greater goal is kept in mind.

The common perception of juggling as a frivolous hobby for kids makes it a difficult career to build a lucrative business around, so if I can do it with juggling, I am certain you can brand **your** passion to create the career of your dreams. If all of this seems daunting, just remember: I juggle plungers.

About the Author

 Jeff Civillico is a Las-Vegas based headline entertainer who blends his perfected art of juggling with friendly audience interaction and insane amounts of energy. With his "Comedy in Action" show, he has performed everywhere from Australia and New Zealand to The White House. He is a favorite onboard Disney Cruise Line, and his credits on the Las Vegas Strip include *V: The Ultimate Variety Show*, *Nathan Burton*, and *The Improv at Harrah's*. In addition to his comedy show, Jeff also delivers a powerful keynote that illustrates the keys to "Branding Your Passion" to create the career, and lifestyle, of your dreams. A 2005 honors graduate of Georgetown University, Jeff currently serves as President of the Georgetown Alumni Club of Las Vegas. He is the Founder and President of *Win-Win Entertainment*, a non-profit that pairs performers willing to donate their time and talent with charities in need of entertainment.

Jeff Civillico may be contacted via:
www.jeffcivillico.com

Follow Your Heart

MARY MONAGHAN

'You should write your story.'

I heard that so many times when I told my story to friends and acquaintances. It was indeed an interesting story...that of the perfect marriage and a husband who went backpacking for three months in Australia never to return. It wasn't as simple as that. I had never written a book before; I didn't know where to start. How would I put it all together? I tried hard to put it out of my mind. The more I tried, the more thoughts of writing my story whirled around in my head. Why not? Even if I wrote it just for myself, it was something new to try, a project. Besides, my story might help other people understand that despite terrible things happening in your life, you can overcome them. I had searched for my missing husband, John, for six long years, never knowing if he was alive or dead. There came a point when I needed to choose to move on with my life. My book *Remember Me?* is a story of survival and new beginnings. I had a vision of what I wanted to achieve. I could see the finished book in bookstores. I had even decided on the cover, a painting that I had commissioned a few years previously of my house by the sea. It was simply a case of turning my dream into reality.

I started attending the Women's Writing Workshops in Cape Town and began to understand the practical aspects of writing a book. It took time; I had no idea how much was involved. It was definitely not as simple as I thought, but I kept at it. I worked on my book in the evenings and on weekends. It was tough as I held a senior position in my company; I worked long hours and travelled frequently. It didn't matter, writing a book was my dream and nothing was going to stand in my way. It would help put my past to rest, it would close a devastating chapter of my life, and be a way of putting the last pieces of my life back together after those terrible years. If only I had the time to get it done.

I worked for a global company in their Human Resources department. We had entered into a joint venture with two other companies and I was tasked with helping launch the values of the new company. I conducted workshops around the country explaining these values and helping the staff come up with practical examples of what these meant. There was just one problem; every time I got to the value, 'integrity in word and deed,' I hit a wall. No one in the company believed the leaders were subscribing to this value. Too many things had happened to too many people.

It was disheartening. Even as I raised this issue with our senior leadership, no one was prepared to listen. I felt that remaining with this company was compromising my integrity. Yes, I could continue to work there, but was that simply selling my soul for money? I needed a job, there was no question. I was a single person responsible for earning my own money. What was more important? Feeding and clothing myself or being able to look at myself in the mirror every morning? I chose to retain my self-respect, leave my job, and take a chance on my own.

Yes, I was scared. The security of a steady income was gone. I tried to think of the freedom I was gaining to do new things. Instead of looking at this as something negative I chose to see the exciting possibilities it brought. Now I would have time to finish my book, publish it, and share my story with others. I was being given the opportunity to reach for my dream. It was difficult at first, waking up in the morning not having any set times to be anywhere, no meetings to attend. Very soon all that changed. I had my book to finish, then the editor and book designer and distributor to see. I had the time to give this baby of mine all the attention it deserved.

It was a proud day when I launched my book, surrounded by many special friends. I held launches in Johannesburg and Cape Town. I shared my story with people through radio, TV, newspaper and magazine articles. My life started to change. I was a published author, someone who could speak out on the ability of women to survive and embark on new life journeys. I started to feel that I was making a difference. The satisfaction it gave me was so much greater than any corporate accolades.

I was doing something I loved. My passion and enthusiasm for what I did rubbed off on other people. They, too, became excited about the possibilities they had in their lives and I was happy to have shown them this path. I made a choice to move out of a regimented and stifling working environment to one which was less stable, less financially secure but with the aim of bringing me more fulfillment and joy. Yes, times could be tough, but if you asked me the questions, "Are you loving life, are you loving what you do?" I can honestly say, "Absolutely!"

Even if times seem hard and uncertain, look for what excites you, what inspires you, and work with that. If you follow your heart, you will always get where you want to go. Leaving a job can be terrifying It can also be an opportunity to rebuild your life, to explore new horizons. You can be anything you choose to be; all it takes is belief in yourself and the energy and passion to pursue your dream.

I eventually found my husband after six long years of searching. When I spoke to him on the telephone, I realized that I was a very different woman from the one he had left behind. Writing my book was a form of liberation from the past and the hold he had over me. He was no longer part of my life. I had moved on. However, there was no question that despite everything I had gone through, there was still a place in my heart for him.

John and I both had roots in Ireland; he was from Donegal and my parents were from Mayo. A year after publishing my book in South Africa, I made the decision to look at publishing it in Ireland. I anticipated a limited response, but wanted my friends and family there to also have access to my story. An article was sent to the Irish newspapers and the response I received was totally unexpected. My story appeared the next day in several national newspapers. I was invited to appear on television and radio shows. I had been between jobs for quite some time and funds were at a low. I calculated very carefully if a trip was going to be worth it. It was a twelve hour flight from Cape Town; being there even for a few days would be expensive. I weighed that up against the opportunity of doing a book signing in my parents' home town, Ballinrobe in County Mayo, being interviewed on Irish national radio and TV stations. I figured it would be a once-in-a-lifetime opportunity. How proud my parents would be to see me do this. I knew I would probably never get another chance like this again. I took a deep breath, paid for the air ticket with my credit card, and left for Ireland the next week. I felt in my heart it was the right decision to make.

Little did I know that the choice I made would turn my life on its head. My last-minute decision to travel to Ireland from South Africa meant that I would be in the country at exactly the same time that my ex-husband, John, would be visiting from Australia. Neither of us had any idea that we were planning to be in Ireland at exactly the same time. It had been fourteen years since I had seen him and eight years since I had spoken to him on the phone. He did not know that I had written a book and was just there for a brief holiday.

When he arrived in Donegal, he heard via the grapevine that I would be in his hometown delivering books to the local bookstore. He decided to surprise me and try to explain why he had vanished all those years ago. When I saw him on the street, it was like seeing a ghost. As he walked toward me on that summer's day in Ballyshannon, I put my hands up to my face, turned my back on him, and stood rooted to the ground. I couldn't walk; I couldn't speak. Eventually, I regained my composure and we went to the lounge of the local hotel where we sat like two strangers, struggling to make conversation.

My decision to take a chance and make the trip helped me finally close this chapter of my life. I sat across the table from him and realized that I was definitely over this man. Seeing him so unexpectedly was emotional—I was overwhelmed, teary-eyed—but not for one minute did I feel the need to touch him, to hug him. He had become a stranger to me; we had followed totally different paths and my life no longer had any space for him.

I was so glad I had made the trip. No longer would I wonder how I would react when I saw John. I knew. But even more came out of this meeting. The story of our chance meeting was picked up in my TV interview a few days later and led to an unexpected wave of publicity. My books started to sell like hotcakes; my story had touched the hearts of so many people. I was so thankful that I had taken the chance and made the journey. Difficult as our meeting was, it laid to rest so many demons. I was no longer afraid of the hold John might have over me. I was my own person. He did not deserve to be part of my life. Our meeting gave me the gift of another book, *Who Do You Belong To?* which chronicles how the writing of *Remember Me?* changed the direction of my life.

My writing journey led me to make many choices, the most important one being to follow my dream despite the hardships and uncertainty it might bring. I made many other choices along the way: the choice to expose my very private story to public view and subject myself to scrutiny; the choice to leave a well-paying job so as not to compromise my integrity; the choice to go to Ireland to promote my book because it felt like the right thing to do. In all my choices, I followed my heart and the path those choices took me on was one that changed my life. I firmly believe that life often turns out the way it is supposed to. I now understand that I just need to relax and let life lead me where it will. There is a plan; I just don't always know what it is until it is revealed to me.

About the Author

Mary Monaghan lives in Cape Town, South Africa, and travels frequently to Europe and the United States, though her roots are in Ireland.

As well as being a writer, Mary is a speaker and also facilitates change and leadership development interventions. She has a passion for helping people develop themselves to be the very best they can be.

Mary is the author of *Remember Me?* (Melkbosstrand, South Africa; Tortoise Press, 2006), which she has adapted into a screenplay. She has also been published in *Writing the Self: An Anthology of New Writing from Women's Writing Workshops* (Muizenberg, South Africa; Women's Writing Workshops, 2008); *Life Choices: Navigating Difficult Paths* (Las Vegas; Turning Point International, 2010); *The Ultimate Runner: Stories and Advice to Keep You Moving* (Deerfield Beach, FL; HCI Books, 2010); and *Who Do You Belong To?* (Melkbosstrand; Tortoise Press 2010).

Mary has a passion for traveling and exploring new places, spending time with friends and family, and enjoying the great outdoors.

Mary Monaghan may be contacted via:
www.marymonaghan.com
marymonaghan@telkomsa.net
P.O. Box 163, Melkbosstrand, 7437, South Africa
+27 83 625 9470

Stage Time

DARREN LACROIX

Why wouldn't you pursue your passion? I mean besides the fear of failure, the fear of success, ridicule by friends, the voice of doubt, and people thinking you are crazy. Listen to a guy with no talent, no chance, and everyone in his life telling him to give it up, who did it anyway.

After four years of business school, my dreams of owning and running ten sandwich shops faded quickly. Forget trying to thrive, I was just trying to survive. I was working in my sandwich shop from 9 a.m. to 1 a.m., seven days per week. I got a second part-time job with a flexible schedule in order to be able to pay my employees. I moved back home with my parents.

Knowing my struggles, my friend gave me a motivational tape by Brian Tracy. I was stunned when I heard Brian pose a question: "What would you dare to dream if you knew you wouldn't fail?" I thought, *I'd be a comedian. How cool would that be earning a living making people laugh? That would be the ultimate.*

Then the voice of reason in my head spoke loud and clear: *What? You are not funny!* Ah, correct, but that wasn't the question. The question was, "What would you dare to dream if you knew you wouldn't fail?"

How would you answer that one? Seriously, consider it. It may just be the key to pinpointing your passion.

How ironic that was for me. I was a quiet, shy kid. I was never considered "funny," never mind the class clown. That was my brother and my cousin, not me.

Listening to motivation programs felt good. This constant stream of mind-expanding ideas was foreign to me, exciting and scary all at the same time. Exciting because of how big I could dream, scary because Brian Tracy was canceling out all the excuses it took me years to accumulate.

My goal at this point became to try stand-up comedy once. Just once. As scared as I was to even consider it, what scared me more was the thought that I might look back later in life and ask myself, *What if? What if I did try it and it worked?*

That was scary. Does the regret of "*What if*" scare you? I hope so!

I decided I was going to try it once, but I was going to go all out. The only thing worse than never trying it, was the thought of trying it half-heartedly and still wondering later in life, *What if I had given it my all?*

I wanted to become a comedian, but who would I go to for advice? A comedian? Sure, it sounds logical. I went to my family. I'm very fortunate. I have a great family and friends who love and care about me. When I told them of my intent, ironically, they laughed. They tried to talk me out of it. In their minds, they compared me to Jerry Seinfeld, but comparing someone at the top of his field to someone just thinking about it is not a fair comparison. It is human nature. They thought they knew what it took to be successful; that to be a comedian, you had to "be funny." Yet they had never been to a comedy club, never met a comedian, and had no real life frame of reference. I probably would have thought the same thing.

One of the best things I did right was not listen to them. Instead, I decided to ask a comedian for advice. Not knowing any, I headed to a comedy club that Friday night.

After the show, I approached one of the comedians, Chris. He asked, "Are you funny?" I replied honestly, "Nope." He said that was okay. "*Really?*" He had my attention. He said no one is funny in the beginning. *Really?* Now, I became a sponge. He gave me two bits of advice.

He said, "Number one, you need to get the book." *Book? There is a book about becoming a comedian?* Well, of course there is a book. There are books about everything; it just didn't dawn on me. He told me to get Judy Carter's *Stand-up Comedy, the Book.* Even if you are not a great "student," if it is your passion, the learning and studying will be fun and exciting. If not, it probably is not your true passion.

Number two, he said—"Go to an open mic night." Watch an amateur night. This *was genius.* What he was doing was getting me to compare myself to someone else just starting out. This was the opposite of what my family was thinking.

Sunday night I went to the comedy club, *Stitches,* right near Fenway Park in Boston. I walked in to the little smoke-filled club and watched people go up on stage for the first time. They were horrible. It was painful to watch. They inspired me. I was going to give it a shot for sure.

I studied for two months. I read the book. I did all of the exercises. I went to *Stitches* every Sunday night for two months. Then it was D Day—my night—April 26th, 1992. I brought friends with me for the main purpose of making sure I did not chicken out. My friend's wife was there with a video camera. I wanted proof that I attempted stand-up comedy once.

Did you ever have a moment in your life that turns into slow motion? This was that moment for me. I will always remember the comedian host introducing me for the first time: "Ladies and gentleman, please welcome to the stage for the first time, Darren LaCroix!" said Vinnie Favorito.

It was a blur. I remember the pain of my punch lines not working. I remember most the moment where I was telling a joke about Dr. Robert Goddard, the first rocket scientist. He had launched the first liquid fueled rocket in history in my hometown. I talked about his first launch and how the rocket took off and went vertically. When I said this, I motioned in a horizontal fashion. It was brutal. I messed up. I said one thing, and I did the exact opposite. I realized my mistake and just reacted. I was disgusted with myself and cried, "Oh s#@t!"

Everyone laughed! I loved that feeling. They were not laughing at my punch line, but instead at my own reaction to my mistake. I finished my five minutes mostly hearing the sounds of the ceiling fan after my punch lines. That was the only laugh I got that night. As I walked off stage, a comedian put his arm around my shoulder in support and said, "Don't worry man. It's just your first time." I questioned, "Just my first time? Did you see what I did? I got a laugh. No one ever told me I could do this."

Why do we let other people tell us what "success" is? Everyone there that night thought I bombed. I looked at it differently. I got a laugh! In those five minutes of time, I had one thing that worked. If I could get rid of everything that didn't work, and figure out how to reproduce the one thing that did, I could do this! I've been on stage making people laugh ever since.

I was hooked. I wanted more of the laughs. I committed to do whatever it took to become a comedian. It didn't matter how long it would take. I was out to pursue my passion. Making people laugh.

What was the best thing I had going for me?

Being clueless! I *knew* that I did not *know.* I was comfortable with being clueless. I was an eager student. To truly pursue your passion you need to be a sponge! Being humble and taking in what mentors teach you helps you grow faster.

My brother is a pilot. As soon as he saved up the money, he went to ground school in Florida to learn from one of the best, a teacher who had logged thousands of hours flying. My brother told me it was one of the best things he ever did. After getting their pilots' license, most aviators go immediately for their instructors' license. They do this so that students will pay for some of their own expensive flight time.

Think about that. You are learning from someone who recently got his or her own pilot's license. He is just a half step ahead of you. Does that make sense? He can't teach from years of wisdom.

I took every class I could; I sought after the best mentors. I know that when I coach speakers, I see things much differently than I did just a few years earlier. Why would you learn from someone just a little ahead of you? That is why I went to comics who had logged thousands of hours of stage time. Who can you go to that has years of experience in your passion?

My mentors came in many forms and each relationship was different. They all shaped me and my progress. The one habit that rose to the top as most important to comedians was "stage time." I was told any day that I did not get on stage was a day I did not grow. Though at the time I did not understand it, I was smart enough to listen and heed the advice. Are you? Are you willing to apply mentors' advice without completely understanding why?

Quite often if I could not get "stage time" in Boston, I would drive two and-a-half hours to Portland, Maine to go on stage for five minutes for free and drive back, and go to my day job the next morning. When one of my high school buddies heard I was doing this he told me I was stupid.

I get paid very well for making people laugh. It has taken me to Malaysia, Singapore, Taiwan, Australia, and Abu Dhabi. I do what I love for a living. Now that same friend looks at me and tells me I'm lucky. Lucky? Apparently you can go from stupid to lucky. If anyone has ever called you stupid, keep going—you are on the right path! Luck is just around the corner!

When pursuing your passion, find out what the most important habits are and commit to them. Listen closely to those with successful experience. Don't let anyone who doesn't understand the habits talk you out of them.

For your passion, find out what your "stage time" is. Then commit to doing it.

In my pursuit of stage time, I started realizing that the key to success was making more mistakes. The more often I got up on stage, the more I would fail, the faster I would grow.

I eventually sold my sandwich shop at a loss. While I figured out what I was going to do with my life, I decided to make my part-time job at Bose Corporation a full-time job as a telemarketer. Though I had a B.S. in finance and marketing, and could have easily advanced in the company and earned a bigger paycheck, instead I stayed at my entry level position to use my flexible schedule to my advantage.

When sitting at my desk at Bose, I came across the company newsletter. In the newsletter was an article about Toastmasters. Curious and clueless, I read the article. As I read, I was thinking, *Hey, comedy clubs are only open at night. Here is a place I could get 'stage time' during the day. I could fail twice a day.*

I was so excited. I walked into the club meeting and noticed something different from the comedy clubs right away. These people were warm, encouraging, and sober. So I went out and joined four Toastmasters clubs. I wanted to quadruple my failure rate. When it is a passion, you should be willing to fail to get where you want to be.

Through Toastmasters, I found the National Speakers Association. I stumbled upon the world of professional speaking. I thought, *Wow, you mean I don't have to be as funny, the audiences are welcoming, and I will earn ten times as much? I'm in!*

I quickly discovered a new passion that I didn't know existed. That clarity fueled my passion. I also discovered something about myself. I enjoyed the laughter, but was driven even more by inspiring people. This became a bigger goal which I would never have discovered had I not pursued my passion. Though I changed direction, I'm thankful for the path I took, and now was uniquely qualified to become more successful, faster. I transitioned out of comedy and put my efforts into becoming a professional speaker. I went from humor being my message to humor being the medium to my message.

Don't limit yourself. When a new or different avenue finds you, consider embracing it. Trust your feelings. Differentiate between the feeling of being scared because it is new and different or being scared because of what others may think of you. Stay on path with your passion, while considering an even bigger and better path for yourself. At the end of your life, you will be lying on your deathbed, not someone else's.

It took me nine years to be an overnight success. There were so many lessons that I learned along the way. After each mountain I climbed, there was another. Enjoying getting to the top of each one is what pursuing your passion is all about.

Though I competed in Toastmasters speech contests several times, on August 25th, 2001 in front of 2000 people in Anaheim, California, I was one of nine finalists out of a field of 25,000 competitors from fourteen countries. *Stitches* seemed like a lifetime ago, and at the same time not that long ago. I never became a headline comedian. Instead, I found something better for me, and yet still make people laugh.

Thanks to many mentors, years of stage time, and more bombs than I could count, I was fortunate enough to become the World Champion of Public Speaking. I got eighteen laughs in a seven-and-a-half minute speech. I was doing what I love to do, inspiring people with my story and making them laugh at the same time. I loved every laugh. Those laughs were beautiful, second only to the ones I hear in my next presentation. That original thought from Brian Tracy's question: I was finally on track to my success in many people's eyes. I was making people laugh, though I was not a comedian.

Winning the World Championship did amazing things for my self-confidence, but not enough. I won just two weeks before September 11, 2001, a day that got most of us to re-evaluate our lives, myself included.

I had two coaches who helped me win the contest. I could not have done it without them. In October I got a call telling me that one of my coaches, Dave McIlhenny, had suddenly died. Ouch. Then a co-worker and fellow Toastmaster, Brad, visited my office cube. He asked me when I was going to leave Bose and pursue speaking full time. I had been telling Brad and other friends for four years that I would quit in January. He asked me again what I was waiting for. I replied, "I can't leave Bose; it's my safety net."

Brad looked me dead in the eye and said, "Darren, Bose is not your safety net. It is your drag net."

Ouch! He was right. The reasons I was not quitting, were the exact reasons I needed to quit. I gave a forty-eight hour notice at Bose. I was gone within one day.

My friends were now very supportive. They asked what they could do to help me. I replied, "Save me a place at the dinner table because I'm not sure I'll have enough money to eat."

I had been spending thirty hours a week selling the Bose music systems. It was time to spend that same time selling myself and building my career. At the time, my self-published book, *Laugh & Get Rich*, which I had leveraged on my credit cards (I don't recommend) was in hand.

I gave myself a year to "make it," even if I had to continue living with my parents and barely scrape by. I never looked back.

Jimmy cracked up at his own joke.

"Remember last year, Jim?" Tim challenged. "Your fur got pretty saggy. One thing we know for sure. If you don't learn from your mistakes, you'll always get another chance."

Jimmy rolled over in the tall grass. "You're just a grump," he yawned. "Relax and feel that nice, warm sun."

"Not until I find the right spot for these nuts," Tim declared.

"Oh, bother," Jimmy grumbled, reluctantly tagging along. "Nuts to the nuts already." He smiled at his own play on words.

"You gotta care about something, Jim," Tim asserted. "I care about nuts."

"I know—we've been through this before," Jimmy sighed. "Writers write."

"Dancers dance," Tim added.

"Singers sing," Jimmy tacked on.

"The problem is that they don't," Tim corrected. "Most do second things first, leave their passion for last."

"Passion, smashion," Jimmy rhymed, making up a word. "What does that mean anyway?"

"It's not that complicated," Tim shared. "Kind of like three words in one, PASS-I-ON. It means that what is most important to me, I want to pass forward, like growing a mighty oak because I care about nuts."

"Well, that makes me the king of the rays," quipped Jimmy, glancing up at the sun.

"Yeah," chuckled Tim. "And all writers write bestsellers in their minds."

"Man, you're on a roll, Tim," Jimmy moaned. "We're all equal, y'know, naked inside our own coat."

"Sure," Tim continued. "And no mother thinks her own baby squirrels are ugly. Doesn't mean they'll ever amount to anything. Somehow we have to figure out that we're not just a big bag of fur—go do something."

"Puppies don't bark at parked cars," Jimmy started again.

"Can't make a comeback if you've never been anywhere," Tim played along.

"Every dud knows a stud."

"On the way or in the way."

"In a hole, stop digging."

"Only dead fish swim with the stream."

"Sometimes you're the pigeon," Jim began ...

"And sometimes the statue," Tim finished.

"Sometimes the dog ..."

"And sometimes the hydrant..."

Jimmy tugged his friend's tail. "Sometimes you feel like a nut," he sang, bursting into laughter.

"Sometimes you don't," Tim chuckled along.

~ Author's Postscript

As we pursue our passions, whatever they may be, remember that a smile is a tiny curve that sets a lot of things straight. If you see someone in need of a smile, please give them yours. That includes you.

About the Author

Author, speaker, and serial entrepreneur, Ridgely Goldsborough ("Richeli" in Spanish), has written nine books, produces a column entitled, "A View From The Ridge" and is the creator of Modest To Millions, a program that chronicles the principles of prosperity, success, and wealth accumulation according to successful self-made individuals.

Ridgely began writing as the publisher of the *Upline Journal*, a monthly periodical. He founded *Network Marketing Lifestyles* magazine, distributed by Time-Warner and *Domain Street* magazine, the first publication of the domain names industry.

As a partner in LightSpeed Unlimited, Ridgely has been immersed in all phases of internet marketing, including website development, user interface, affiliate marketing, SEO and sales conversions, with an emphasis on speed to market.

Ridgely holds a BA from the University of Virginia, a JD from Whittier College School of Law and a Master Writers' Certificate from UCLA. He lives in Florida with his wife, Kathy, and their four children.

Ridgely Goldsborough may be contacted via:
ridgelyg@gmail.com
www.AViewFromTheRidge.com
www.Richeli.com (Spanish)
16268 North Shore Drive
Pensacola, Florida 32507
(850) 291-6575

Acceptance

Never underestimate the power of passion.

—*Eve Sawyer*

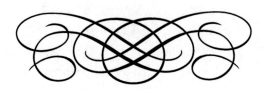

Making the Decision to Forgive

DR. DALLAS HUMBLE

Inside each of us lies a part of ourselves that most never develop; a part that drives us with passion in life that only few portray. The sad part is that although we all have this innate "super self" within us, which I call "the seed planted by God," some do not make a decision to water and nurture it to its full growth. Without letting go of yesterday, however, this giftedness can never be developed, and passion and joy for life today achieved. Regardless of possessions acquired within the materialistic world, if the underlying principles are not understood—strategies and concepts that lead to a fulfilling, more organized life—happiness will not be found.

As we strive to achieve success in life, we must first confront and forgive past mistakes and those who have wronged us. Forgiveness can be one of the most difficult steps toward having the life we desire. Without our past failures, we would not be all that we can be. Without the mistakes I made and the failures I have experienced, I probably wouldn't be writing and sharing this with you, nor would I have achieved any of the successes life has brought my way. More importantly, I wouldn't appreciate them the way I do today. Without life's lessons, we would never learn right from wrong or good from bad. Children may be told repeatedly not to touch a hot stove, but unfortunately, words are nothing like experience. As the child goes against the words, carrying through with actions, the lesson learned will never be forgotten.

Like children learning right from wrong, we venture forth doing as we are told, taught, read to, preached to, and guided to do. Life's choices often do not fit into the box we were given. Each circumstance is different, the people involved are different, and we are different. What others have seen and done may be important, but the choices that face us are unique and we must make decisions now for the choices that will surely come our way later. General Colin Powell, whose leadership helped win the Gulf War known as "Desert Storm," once wrote the following:

There are no secrets of success. Don't waste time looking for them. Success is the result of perfection, hard work, learning from failure, loyalty to those for whom you work, and persistence.

We can view our past in one of two ways: with bitterness or forgiveness. Choosing bitterness causes internal bleeding; we may become bitter toward God, toward our families, loved ones, jobs, or the world in general. In essence, bitterness spreads toward everything and everyone we come in contact with, creating failures from our failures.

Forgiving past mistakes and accepting them as life lessons will bring a peace over us that others will see and which may cease creating more failures from our past mistakes. Unforgiving, bitter individuals blame others for their mistakes, believing life owes them a favor. The unforgiving individual carries the deposits of life indefinitely.

People walk in and out of our lives daily leaving deposits, much like a bird that flies over, drops a deposit on our noses, and flies away. We can wash our faces, forgive the bird and go on, or we can leave the deposit prominently affixed to our noses for the entire world to see and before long people will start avoiding us. We can either forgive the bird or hold a grudge for the rest of our lives. People are much like this, carrying the deposits of life, layering them one after the other. Before long no one cares to be near them. Are you one of these people? Do you hate seeing others' success, scoff at new ideas, laugh at others, and discourage all who come in contact with you? If you have not realized the gift of forgiveness, others may view you that way. It is my desire for you to free yourself from your past mistakes or failures and take the first step toward achieving true prosperity in your life.

Forgiving individuals look inside themselves and accept responsibility for their own actions, allowing failures to make them better people. Unforgiving individuals are quick to anger, quick to speak, and often allow hatred and condemnation to build up on the inside. Forgiving individuals have inner peace, peace with others, and most importantly peace with God. They have a love for others, are slow to anger, slow to speak, and slow to point a finger at others. These individuals can be described in James 1:19: "My dear brothers, take note of this: Everyone should be quick to listen, slow to speak and slow to become angry." Forgiveness allows thankfulness; we remain alive and opportunities lie ahead of us. As good and right as it is, however, forgiveness is one of the most difficult things to achieve. There are countless stories of forgiveness, but all have a common denominator—freedom. Forgiveness grants freedom from the past that translates to a more fulfilled and prosperous future.

I spent a great deal of my life trying to understand why something so right is so difficult. Sure, we say the right things in life are never easy; just bite the bullet and go on. Although sayings such as this may be true, they do not help people learn to "let go." The question often arises, "Why do some individuals become successful in spite of overwhelming odds?" Some overcome physical handicaps, poverty, abuse, etc., while others have everything going for them and never really reach their life's potential.

What is the key difference between individuals born of the same family, having the same opportunities, brought up in the same environment, where one goes astray, while the other strives for success? They both made mistakes and experienced failures in life, and perhaps both say they forgave their past. If this is the case and with the choice obviously being ours, what is the key difference? Maybe one didn't really forgive. It isn't the environment in which they were raised. What are the key factors? You have heard it before and I hope to explain it in an understandable manner. Without question, the keys are accepting full responsibility for your actions, making the decision to forgive yourself and others, and creating a positive attitude about life in general. Without releasing yesterday and taking responsibility for today, we will never reach our full potential. Forgiving everyone, including ourselves, for failure is difficult to say the least, but one way to accomplish this is by maintaining a healthy attitude. The importance of attitude can be summed up in the following description:

The longer I live, the more I realize the importance of a good attitude. It is more important than money, earthly possessions, education, success and/or attainments. It is more important than your physical appearance or your skills. It will make or break everything from a company to a home. We cannot change the past, present, or future, but we can change the way it is viewed and by doing so affect the way we are viewed. In reality, attitude is the very essence of the hows and whys of life. When asked how something was accomplished, attitude is a major factor. When asked, "why him or her and not me," attitude is the major factor. Although I cannot change the inevitable, I am convinced that life is more how I react to it than what happens to me. You are in charge of your attitude and therefore you are in charge of your life. Attitude is not something to be taken lightly.

Some people lose loved ones in ways that could cause the most positive-thinking person to become negative, but instead they choose to serve God and mankind even more. They express their love for others in ways not dreamed possible prior to their tragedy. Yes, they grieved, and could have become bitter as well, but they chose forgiveness. Grieving the loss of loved ones is normal, it cleanses the soul, but regardless of the tragedy, it doesn't have to turn into bitterness, hatred, or condemnation.

My past has been filled with mistakes and failures that would have caused many to throw in the towel. My reason for not giving up was hardly my own strength; as a man, I am weak. My faith, a persistent never-give-up attitude and the realization that the two bookmarks to success are "Starting" and "Finishing" got me through. We will not have until we start and it is not over until we are finished.

My attitude on life is my choice; I must first make the decision to have the right attitude, let go of yesterday, and quit blaming others for my failures or deficiencies. Once that decision is made, there remains no further choice in the matter. I am one hundred percent responsible for my actions. You may be saying, "But it wasn't my fault." Fault doesn't matter; your response is your responsibility. Your future and success begin with closing the door on the past. When past mistakes cause you to think of failure rather than success, you remain anchored to the past. Anchoring happens when an event or person is associated with good or bad; close the door and walk away, taking with you only the learning experiences, not the mistakes themselves, or you will never reach your desired success in life. In forgiving my past and those involved, my bitterness diminished and as my bitterness diminished, my problems seemed less "life threatening."

I had every reason to hate people, hold grudges, and retaliate. I have personally witnessed people retaliate for small infractions. People have come to the point of verbal abuse because it is the world's way... unforgiving, non-understanding, retaliating in greater measure. You must be different and realize that true forgiveness through total surrender to a higher power will lead you to achieve success in life. At times, I find myself praying for those whom I once couldn't bear to think about, much less talk about. Forgiveness really is a difficult decision that can't be achieved alone. No matter how big the obstacle or how impossible it may seem, forgiveness is possible; I know because I did it myself.

You, too, may be battling with your past. It doesn't matter whether your past is filled with mistakes to the point of feeling like a total failure, whether you came from poverty or abuse. When you are willing to submit your pride and work, anything is possible. A regretful past is usually discussed with phrases such as "Hindsight is twenty-twenty" or "If only I knew then what I know now, I would ..." These phrases do nothing to further the healing process so necessary to put our past mistakes behind.

Gain mastery over the tendencies toward retaliation. Don't conform to the world or be overcome by evil, but overcome evil with good. The only way to get past resentment, revenge, rage, or retaliation and have the life you desire is forgiveness. Realize that anger is only one letter away from danger, like a cancer that will eat you up on the inside. Close the door and move forward. Without doing so, the true joy and peace that life can hold for you will never be experienced. Make the decision today to forgive when wrong comes your way; you will not only experience true joy, but you will also be on your way to achieving the successful life you desire.

About The Author

Dr. Dallas Humble is an entrepreneur, author, speaker and success/wellness coach teaching others how to live life at its highest level. He has served as CEO of several successful businesses, written numerous articles published in professional journals on business management, wellness, and success strategies and has authored numerous books and recordings sold worldwide.

Often known for his *Make It Happen* and *Peak Performance Strategies*, Dr. Humble has been featured in several personal development films and recordings including *The Journey*, a movie documentary with Brian Tracy and Bob Proctor. He is one of the most highly sought-after motivational speakers in America, delivering positive inspirational messages of hope, faith, belief, and a winning attitude to those with whom he comes in contact. Dr. Humble is available to speak to groups, churches or organizations on any of these subjects. For more information, visit www.makeithappennetwork.com.

Dallas Humble may be contacted via:
MIH Ventures, LLC
355 Carey Nelson Road
West Monroe, LA 71292
(318) 397-9680
drh@dallashumble.com

What's Behind Your 'Perfect Mask?'

CHARLYN SHELTON

Some may call them coincidences, happenstance, or even serendipity. I call them "God's little miracles."

The first 'coincidence' in my life-changing journey happened in August 2006. As a business owner, I have always believed in investing in myself to be the best I can be. Jack Canfield, co-creator of the *Chicken Soup for the Soul* series, was the keynote speaker at the Buffini Mastermind Conference I attended in San Diego. At the end of his session, Jack was meeting with anyone who wanted him to autograph his book. I waited in line along with hundreds of others to be able to have a moment to speak face-to-face with him. I didn't want an autograph. I wanted to say 'thank you.' Twenty years prior, I had attended 'Self-Esteem and Peak Performance,' a one-day training in Kansas City which Jack presented that had changed the direction of my life forever. I wanted to let him know what a difference he'd made in my life. I knew famous authors spoke in front of thousands of people every year and one face can tend to fade into the next, but for some reason that nagging little voice in my heart said I must speak to him. (You know that voice...the one that won't leave you alone even though you argue with it.)

When it was finally my turn to approach him, I wanted to turn and run. I thought for sure he would think I was nuts. *Why would he even care?*

"Mr. Canfield, I just wanted to say you thank you for making a difference in my life over twenty years ago. After attending your one-day seminar in Kansas City, I bought the cassette tapes of 'Self-Esteem and

Peak Performance' and listened to them over and over and over again. As a matter of fact, I even had to write the company and get another copy of tape #9, the affirmations tape, because I wore out the first one."

He smiled his million-dollar smile, thanked me politely, and said, "I have something better coming soon; give me your card and I'll make sure you hear about it."

I thanked him and hurriedly left the convention center, all the while thinking how embarrassed I was for making a fool of myself and that I would never hear from him again. However, in just a few short weeks, I was getting emails on a regular basis regarding all of his events and trainings.

In April 2007, I experienced God's little miracle number two. I received an email about a one-week training program that Jack was offering in Scottsdale, Arizona, entitled, 'Breakthrough to Success,' to be held in July of that year. After much inner debate whether or not I should go, whether or not I should take that much time off of work, whether or not I could afford it (you know the drill), I committed to attend. (There was a 100 percent money-back guarantee, so what the heck!) The worst-case scenario would be that I have a one-week 'vacation' in the middle of July in the desert where the temperature reaches 115 degrees! As a travel agent for twenty-five years, the irony of this rationalization was not lost on me!

I arrived at the Fairmont Hotel in Scottsdale—late, exhausted—and tried to check in along with the other 400 people from twenty-eight different countries. The lines were long, people were crowded into the lobby, and the hotel was sold out. I finally got my turn at the front desk, gave the clerk my name and reservation number. The clerk smiled politely and told me my reservation was for the *next* night. (No, I didn't tell her that I was an owner of a travel agency, nor that I was the one who had booked the reservation.) Instead, I blamed it on 'the absentee' travel agent. The front desk clerk worked hard and was able to secure a conference room with a fold-out couch for that first night. (Yet another little coincidence; having a place to sleep in an oversold hotel.)

The conference was amazing. We worked hard for seven straight days, sometimes ten hours a day. I was hooked. It pushed me way beyond my comfort zone. The exercises made me stretch in ways I never had before .... to growth I had never been able to achieve. In addition, I forged lifelong friendships with people from all over the world.

Even with all the learning and stretching, the biggest 'take away' of the conference for me wasn't anything that Jack or any of the other trainers and speakers actually spoke about. It was a simple exercise he had the whole group do first thing every morning: *hug*. To many of you, that might seem like a silly thing to say, but to someone who had grown up in abusive homes her whole life, I didn't like to be touched, much less hugged! First thing every morning, we would walk around the room not saying a word, with soft music playing, and for five minutes we hugged complete strangers. In the beginning of the week, I begrudgingly participated. By day seven, not only had I learned to happily participate in the 'hugging exercise,' I had tears rolling down my cheeks. I was sorry this experience and the accompanying feelings would be ending. I was going back to St. George, Utah, alone to an empty house and my heart had changed 180 degrees. I had learned the true joy of giving and receiving unconditional love!

In November of 2007 on Coronado Island, California, the next level of training was held. This time I was in a group of 150. I was excited to be returning and renewing those relationships! The training was even more intense and I wanted to learn as much as I could to improve my business. The 'experts' say that 95 percent of the population is satisfied with mediocrity or with status quo, while the other 5 percent are the ones who will continue to learn and grow. An old proverb says, 'The cream always rises to the top.' Well, I wanted to be at the top! We enjoyed four wonderful days together learning, stretching, growing, and bonding even more.

After the Advanced Training, the next level to move up with Jack's training was the Platinum Group. There were limited spaces available, forty to be exact, and you had to apply to be accepted into the program. I had no idea how or why; but that little voice was back again telling me I had to do this. So with trepidation, I filled out the paperwork and nervously turned it in. There were many talented, highly successful people in the group. There were doctors, lawyers, accountants, financial planners, and very wealthy business owners.

I felt like I was in way over my head. That little voice kept nagging me to get involved. I nervously handed in my application along with a prayer and waited. I loved all of these people and I wanted more than anything to be 'worthy' to be with them.

Hallelujah, praise the Lord, kiss the floor...another of God's little miracles—I was accepted. Whew! They hadn't seen through to the scared, insecure, unworthy person that I believed I was! The successful corporate business owner façade had worked again.

The last and most significant coincidence happened on Jan. 11, 2008 at the Fairmont Hotel in Newport Beach, California. Little did I know when I woke up that morning that all of the other 'little miracles' had led up to this very day. The Platinum group—forty of us—were meeting with Jack to start our year of training. It was still in the first half of the first day and the entire group was seated in a 'u-shape' formation in a small conference room. The trainer at this particular time was a gentleman named Jim Bunch from the Ultimate Game of Life. We were discussing tolerance and how it affected both our personal and business lives. I was bursting at the seams with a question and I sat there for several minutes debating whether to ask it in front of this formative group. Once again that little voice wouldn't leave me alone! So, I sheepishly raised my hand and asked the question. At that moment Jack was standing at the back of the room...observing. He came up behind me, gently placed both of his hands on my shoulders, and asked me to approach front and center. My heart went to my throat and I froze. I took a deep breath, then slowly walked up and stood in front of this powerful group.

"Now, Charlyn," he said, "just stand here. Don't say a word. The rest of you...tell me what you see."

My mind shouted, "Oh, God, please let the floor open up and swallow me *now*!" But no, I couldn't have been that lucky. The doctor raised her hand and said, "I see someone who probably has several college degrees."

One business owner said, "I see a very successful business owner who runs a multi-million dollar company." A top level graphic designer from New York's reply was, "Because she is tall, blonde, and beautiful, I see a former high-end model who made a ton of money in that career sometime in her life." The best one: "I see a tall, beautiful, blonde married to a rich doctor who's never had to work in her life!"

As I stood there and heard their responses, the 'perfect mask' I had been hiding behind during my entire adult life started to crack. You might know the one, the perfect face some of us present to the public, covering the wounds inside. The tears welled up and gently started rolling down my cheeks. The self-imposed walls were crumbling and the dam burst. I couldn't move. I couldn't speak. I could barely breathe.

Jack, still standing behind me, with his hands on my shoulders, gently encouraged me. "Charlyn, tell them who *you* see."...dead silence..."Go ahead; it's okay ...tell them who *you* see ..."

Jack suggested that I look into their eyes. I slowly raised my head, squared my shoulders, and looked into the eyes of my newly-found friends.

My voice cracked. With my eyes downcast, I whispered, "I see an unwed mother on welfare at the age of seventeen. I hear my father's voice inside my head after I told him I was pregnant: 'Well, you'd better go apply for welfare; that's what I pay my taxes for."

I had a life-changing experience that day as I looked into the faces of these wonderful people. I didn't see disgust or shame or embarrassment. No, just the opposite! All I saw was kindness, caring, and unconditional love! By the end of this experience, there wasn't a dry eye in the place and I received my first standing ovation.

Jack Canfield and the people of Platinum taught me many priceless lessons. I realized I could continue to push hard to succeed as a business owner, keeping the façade, and no one would ever find out who I truly was, like in the past. Or I could embrace the champion within me, change my mission, and follow my passion.

As a little girl, all I wanted was someone to see the hurts that were inside. As an adult, all I wanted was to hide those hurts...until I broke out from behind my 'perfect mask'. My passion now is to help others do the same. Nothing makes me happier than to be able in some small way to show others that they, too, have a champion within. It has nothing to do with being 'worthy.'

As Dr. Maya Angelou says, "When you know better, you do better."

Now, thanks to Jack and those forty wonderful people whose love and friendships have been priceless gifts to me, I have dropped the façade, thrown away my 'perfect mask,' and embraced my life's passion to help others through my speaking and mentoring. My mantra is to give H.O.P.E. (Help in Overcoming Past Experiences) to everyone I meet.

I now realize that God placed all the little 'miracles' in just the right places and at just the right time in order for me to pursue my passion. I also learned that sometimes the hardest words to live by can be, "Thy will be done". Recognizing the 'coincidences' that have been placed on my path to help me find my way and learning to embrace the good as well as the not so good, has actually been the perfect journey. My path was there for me all along, I just had to find my way. We each have our unique journey, our own path. You, too, can drop 'the perfect mask' and embrace the happiness that awaits.

About the Author

Entrepreneur, speaker, consultant and writer Charlyn Shelton has used her unparalleled business background to create a life devoted to helping other women find happiness and success. Charlyn has coined the term "Boomerpreneur." It's time for Baby Boomers to emerge using new business technologies to become the people they were meant to be!

Charlyn's uplifting and loving spirit has almost accidently propelled her into this career after 25 successful years owning her own businesses in both the travel and the real estate industries. Her nurturing nature and the personal obstacles she has overcome have led her down a path that includes: being personally trained by Jack Canfield (co-creator of the *Chicken Soup for the Soul* series), a mastermind group facilitator, workshop leader and personal coach.

Charlyn enjoys spending her time making a difference in people's lives. She is known as the 'Catalyst to Happiness, Wealth and Wellness' to her clients, colleagues and friends. With her humor and her contagious laugh you too will understand why! If you feel like you need help breaking through to the next level of success, Charlyn is the just the catalyst you need!

Charlyn Shelton may be contacted via:
CS Enterprises, Inc.
P.O. Box 470774
Celebration, Florida 34747
(888) 619-4990

The Master Knows Best

ANTHONY SPINICCHIA

It should go without saying that pursuing your passion is a path to a fulfilling life. Most people dream about this life, but unfortunately, not everyone really finds it. Most of us want to pursue our passion, but for various reasons fail to do so. Some people are passionate about a lot of things but are not focused on any particular thing. For some, it takes the vision of someone else important in our lives to motivate us and help us focus on pursuing our passion, for the good of ourselves and others. In my case, it turned out to be my Sifu. This guidance led me to a life of fulfillment that I would never have imagined.

More than ten years ago, I became a faithful student of a world famous Shaolin master, Sifu Wong Kiew Kit. Sifu is a traditional Chinese term for master. I had been having some serious, stress-related health problems and I sought him out at his home in remote northern Malaysia, near the Thai border. He kindly taught me a very rare and exclusive health exercise called Shaolin Chi Kung, and by practicing faithfully, I overcame all of my conditions and achieved much more. The easy, fifteen minute, twice-a-day practice of this special Chi Kung became my passion. It became a deep, meditative time that enriched all other areas of my life, and the lives of others, too.

Chi Kung means 'Art of Energy,' and it has been practiced in many cultures for thousands of years. Shaolin is a mountain in central China, and more famously, the location of the first of several Shaolin temples. This temple was an imperial temple that was sponsored and visited by the emperors of China, usually once a year, as they came to pray on behalf of the people. It was closed and only accessible by the elite of

China including generals, royalty, and others of special attainment. It was a place of cultivation of many special arts including Chi Kung, Kung Fu, and Zen (the more common and famous Japanese word for the Chinese word, Chan). Not many people know that Zen came from Shaolin. The famous Indian prince, Bodhidharma, initiated it there about 1500 years ago. The philosophy of Zen—simple, direct, and effective—was embodied in all Shaolin arts. Bodhidharma also initiated a special style of non-religious Chi Kung, which was jealously guarded and passed down through a lineage of masters to the present.

Shaolin Chi Kung is unfathomably deep and vast in its breadth of useful functions and benefits. It was developed to help special people in their spiritual pursuits and to help elite people of important responsibility function more effectively. Naturally, this included the benefit of reducing and eliminating the bad effects of stress. It also provided increased energy, creativity, problem-solving, and general effectiveness in all areas. It provided robust health on all four levels: the physical, mental, emotional, and spiritual. A traditional Shaolin and Chinese principle is that these four levels of health cannot be disconnected. Making it even more profound, it not only provided an effective way to overcome seemingly incurable illnesses, but more importantly, prevent them, which in Chinese culture is considered a higher level of medicine. This special art had the benefit of refinement by generations of Zen masters to make it especially efficient, enjoyable, and effective. It truly lived up to the description of "The Art of Emperors and Generals."

Within months of daily practice, I overcame all of my health problems and all areas of my life were enriched. Benefits included more energy for my work that left my co-workers both impressed and a little frustrated as they tried to keep up. I began to recognize and invent new applications for my company's products that were needed in the marketplace. This didn't necessarily fall into my area of responsibility as a traveling corporate manager, but it was well received and supported by the company's executive offices.

All of my relationships improved. When one's health becomes robust and stress becomes less of a factor, this is inevitable. My voracious appetite for life grew, seemingly unlocked and fed by this simple, yet very profound, gentle and easy exercise that I did faithfully each day in short ten- to twenty-minute sessions, which I could perform almost anywhere, making it even more convenient.

I looked forward to a life of fun and fulfillment, especially enabled by my special practice. So it came as a big, unwelcome shock when my Sifu "asked" me to become a teacher of Chi Kung. Every master has his own style, and in my teacher's case, as a powerful Zen Master, he simply told me that it was my future. I was going to train under him to be a teacher because it would be rewarding both to me and to many people in the USA who needed the benefits of our special art. Even though this opportunity would be considered a very rare and unimaginable honor, it wasn't what I wanted. The mere thought of it made me very uncomfortable. I simply wanted to be a student and enjoy my life. I didn't want the deep responsibilities of teaching and supporting students of such a powerful art.

Six months later, when I saw my teacher again I begged him to let me avoid becoming a teacher. He kindly smiled and told me, with compassion, not to worry; just forget about it and enjoy my practice. I felt so happy and relieved and continued with my life, surely not realizing that a couple of years later I would finally recognize that it was indeed my destiny and that I would eventually embrace it. Interestingly, I also learned some years later that my own Sifu and my Sigung (my Sifu's Sifu) had reacted similarly when they were informed that they would have these types of responsibilities. This made me feel better knowing that a sincere, from-the-heart reaction of not desiring such powerful responsibilities, which can include spiritual ones, is a typical attribute of good teachers.

In my limited spare time, I slowly began to teach people in need or who had an interest. The reaction and results of the students was amazing and very encouraging to me. Students were able to easily overcome all types of difficult health conditions and live richer, deeper lives of joy and fulfillment.

I felt very happy that I was able to fulfill my Sifu's directive, or so I thought, while still carrying on my life. I had no idea where pursuing my passion would lead me. In some ways I still don't. I never considered that this would lead me to dedicate all my time to this cause, which, after a few years, it did. Eventually I was invited across the country and around the world, from Europe to Asia to Latin America, to teach this special art. This has led me to meet many interesting people and to visit many interesting places. I could never have predicted, and I certainly never expected, that I would meet and teach such a variety of people from beyond the business world like successful artists, authors, entertainment professionals, wonderful couples, retirees of remarkable accomplishment, and many more. The heart-warming and deep sense of satisfaction one receives from contributing to the improvement of people's lives is really significant. To receive feedback from students about how their marriages are improved or how relationships between parents and children are improved is priceless.

Practicing and teaching Chi Kung is my passion. As a Sifu, my interest is always what is best for the student. Even though the results for students are tangible and typically remarkable, the focus of what is best for the student provides a clear and unambiguous goal. There is no room for ego-inflating pursuits, which helps keep one appropriately humble and is good for everyone. In some professions, even if they are passions, the focus may not be there, which can lead to some problems. I'm grateful for the guidelines passed down by many generations of masters to help us keep things in perspective today.

I'm honored by the opportunities to give public lectures on the benefits of our arts to help educate the public on profound Eastern philosophies, including Zen, in which people can broaden their horizons and enrich their own lives from clear explanation, understanding, and practical application. Furthermore, I'm touched when I receive letters from people across the globe telling me how my book, *The Wonders of Chi Kung*, has helped them. I'm confident that my upcoming book, *Ten Years with a Zen Master*, will do the same.

As I've said, I never could have envisioned or predicted this. I never had an interest in New Age practices, a part of which our traditional and time-tested Chi Kung certainly is *not*. I wasn't seeking something that could so powerfully affect people's lives. If you take the step to *pursue your passion,* you'll likely be rewarded in ways that today you can't imagine either.

You may have heard the expression, "The Master knows best." Certainly, in my case, this is true. Pursuing my passion led me to a deeply fulfilling life, and in turn, helping others do the same, as they get more out of life. Please keep an open mind if a respected advisor gives you some guidance to help you pursue *your* passion.

About the Author

 Anthony Spinicchia teaches Shaolin Chi Kung to individuals, groups, and organizations, including customized programs for conferences, as well as conducting public and private lectures on this incredible art and how it is relevant to organizations and people today. He also provides personalized Chi Therapy to help people self-heal from chronic, painful, and life-threatening conditions. Anthony's popular lectures and presentations are known for being informative, interesting, and fun. If you would like a presentation to your group or organization on Shaolin Chi Kung, its Zen approach "simple, direct, and effective" and how it is relevant, or if you are interested in Chi Therapy for yourself or a loved one, contact Anthony Spinicchia.

Anthony Spinicchia may be contacted via:
sifu@elitechikung.com
www.elitechikung.com
www.elitecorporatetraining.com
72 W Horizon Ridge Parkway, 120-191
Henderson, Nevada 89012
(702) 672-9563

The Whispers of My Heart

CHARLOTTE FOUST

Terror. There's no other way to describe it. It started in the pit of my stomach and radiated in stages to the rest of my body. My knees wanted to buckle. My hands shook. My voice cracked and the tears rolled down my cheeks. I was standing in front of my eighth grade English class. It was a simple assignment…memorize a poem and recite it in front of the class. It counted for half of my grade for that semester. I got through the first line before I started to cry. I managed to finish, sniffing and gasping all the way. I vowed I would never speak in front of a group of people again.

I never imagined I would be speaking once, sometimes twice, a week… every week. *Me? No way. I don't speak in public.* A career that involved public speaking was NOT on the top of my "things I most want to do" list. Yet, here I am, serving as Associate Minister at Unity Church of Las Vegas. I present the Wednesday night services and 'platform' most Sundays. When our Senior Minister is not well or taking a planned day off to attend conferences, I lead those services as well.

I wish I could say that I heard the call, entered seminary and came out the other side following my passion. It didn't happen like that. My guess is, I'm not alone. It's a wonderful, romantic notion that when ministers are "called" by God, they not only hear, but also heed the call. Most of the ministers I know reacted in much the same way I did. *Me? Are you sure? Do you know who you're talking to?* While that reaction usually stems from things we know about our pasts which conditioned us to believe God wouldn't be speaking to us much less calling us to action, for me, there was more than a hint of fear involved.

By the time I became aware of the whisper in my heart, I had already made myself the victim of my fears. There were a lot of things I didn't do because I wasn't willing to risk the same kind of humiliation I experienced in the eighth grade. I allowed myself to believe I wasn't capable of succeeding at anything. My fears and tears were my constant companions, their voices so much louder than my desires. I used dancing as an escape. It was the perfect excuse for just about everything. I didn't have time to do anything else. I went straight from school to the dance studio, arriving in time to do a little homework before my first class. Dinner was between classes. By the time I got home, there was time for a little more homework and sleep. Saturdays were filled with dancing, too. I was in control of the demands I made on my body. My mind was only there to remember the steps, not to think. The music helped to drown out the voices inside. I didn't have to feel the pain of failure when I couldn't hear the voices.

Passion is most often thought of as a powerful, driving force pulsing from within, demanding to be acknowledged. Passionate people are described as zealous, driven, enthusiastic, laser focused and unreserved. There was a certain passion to my dancing. I loved the freedom it gave me and how the music felt as I let it flow through me. I loved being in control of my body. I never really liked performing for an audience. I was embarrassed, never believing I was quite good enough. It was a career choice only because I knew how to do it. The term "stage fright" barely explains what I felt at each new audition or opening night. Still, I would have willingly chosen to dance for an audience of thousands before I would agree to speak to a small gathering of people. I didn't realize how many lessons dancing would teach me that I would use much later and in a much different way.

Passion is also quiet, patient and enduring. It is that spark of life deep inside, coaching, cajoling and directing even when we are not aware of its existence. We can bury ourselves in other pursuits, find our way into successful careers and forge relationships without ever consciously acknowledging our true passion. Many of us do. I did. What I know now is that by not listening, not acknowledging the still, small voice inside, my life was filled with road blocks, pitfalls and struggle. I fought for the bits and pieces of self-esteem I managed to muster. I rarely took pride in my work. Yet, through it all, my passion lay dormant…patiently waiting to be discovered, gently guiding me in the direction it would ultimately take me.

I first became aware of my longing to be part of church at an early age. That didn't work out well at all. I had no idea what I was feeling, had no way of expressing it and was afraid to talk about it. We were not a religious family. We didn't attend church. It was never discussed, we simply didn't go. Occasionally, I was invited to go to church with a friend from school. I loved the peace, the familiar feeling of coming home even though I had never been in that building before. I wanted to be invited to go more often, but never asked anyone to take me.

I was living in Las Vegas, dancing in the main room extravaganza "Casino de Paris" at the Dunes Hotel when I started attending church on a somewhat regular basis. My roommate invited me to go to church with her on Sunday. It would be a challenge as we didn't get home from work until almost three a.m. and the service was at 10:00 a.m. It would mean a short night's sleep. We agreed that if we sacrificed sleep to go to church, we would treat ourselves to brunch at our favorite restaurant after service and then go to a movie. I remember how my heart leapt when we walked into the sanctuary for the first time. Even today, I feel that same peaceful feeling whenever I visit that church.

The whispers of my heart were kept at bay by the constant chatter of my life. Even when I acknowledged them, I let my head tell me what it thought my heart was saying. I moved. I married. I went to Australia. I changed careers, more than once, had a child and changed husbands. Restless and unsettled, I bumped along through life, going in no specific direction and ending up nowhere.

A friend of mine was in Las Vegas attending a professional conference. Her conference ended on Saturday night and as it was Easter weekend, we made plans to go to a sunrise service on Mt. Charleston. During breakfast after service, we both expressed our disappointment in the minister's sermon. We were feeling empty and decided we would go to another service at a different church. It was during the meditation at that second service that I heard the voice of my heart, loud and clear. I was called to minister...to bring words of hope, healing and peace into a troubled world. *Me? Remember me? I'm the one who vowed years ago never to speak in public.*

I had no intention of becoming a minister. I knew it would mean speaking in front of people regularly. I allowed my head to translate what my heart was saying. I rationalized that I could take classes, go through ministerial school and placate the longing in my heart...I didn't have to take the final step and commit to being a minister. My spiritual growth would be only for my own benefit. It was 20 more years before I was able to surrender to my passion.

I still experience "stage fright" every time I speak. I often hear the voices in my head telling me I'm not good enough. Studying, attending services and learning to meditate have helped me become quiet long enough to listen to the voice of reason whispering in my heart. This has helped to calm my doubts and fears. My passion is NOT speaking, nor is it writing. My passion is bringing hope, peace and light into the darkened corners of the world. That means I must write and, I must speak. These are the skills I continue to develop in order to free my passion.

A new kind of music flows through me. It is the rhythm of my passion. Gentle and patient, it vibrates within me, pushing me past my self-imposed limitations and giving me a reason to conquer my fears. I make a conscious choice every day to stop and listen to the whispers my heart. Life is less complicated when I do. The bumps in the road are not as rough, the pitfalls not as deep.

My heart no longer whispers. It shouts with a powerful, driving force pulsing from within – demanding to be acknowledged.

About the Author

Though her heart lives in the redwoods of northern California, Charlotte Foust's career as a dancer led her to make Las Vegas her home forty-two years ago. Before becoming executive assistant to a motivational speaker and author, the twists and turns of life took her through successful careers not only as a dancer, but also in sales and marketing, cosmetology, and the title and escrow industry. As the owner/director of a ballroom dance studio, she developed a program of creative and therapeutic dance for the intellectually challenged community of Las Vegas. She has enjoyed countless hours volunteering with Special Olympics, Children's Miracle Network, and numerous local Las Vegas organizations. Driven by the desire to find balance and harmony, she pursued spiritual studies throughout her journey, finally putting her on a path toward the ministry. Charlotte currently serves as associate minister of Unity Church of Las Vegas.

Charlotte Foust may be contacted via:
Rev.Charlotte@live.com

upport

No passion in the world is equal to the passion to alter someone else's draft.

—H. G. Wells

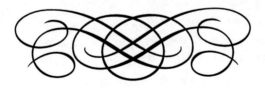

Entrepreneurship: Finding Success through Friendship

CINDI R. MACIOLEK AND JENNA DOUGHTON

"Are you being productive?"

Entrepreneurs know how hard it is to build a business and stay motivated. Not everyone understands what you're doing, including friends and family. Sometimes you turn to them for help or even criticism, but all you get are cheerleaders because they think if they cheer you on, everything will be okay. They don't know how else to support you.

What you truly need is effective and unbiased support. You need your own business coach! We found a way to build a successful support system free of charge (except for a few lunches here and there), and we hope that by sharing what we've done, you, too, will coach your way to business success.

We met through a business connection, and kept in touch. As it turned out, we both yearned to grow our businesses, but found it difficult with the economic circumstances the country faced. Still, we had very optimistic views of what we could contribute to our clients, and we talked about turning off the negativity and creating our own upbeat environment.

As 2008 drew to a close, we were tired of all the doom and gloom. We knew that if we put our hearts and our minds to work, we could make a positive difference in our businesses. We agreed to be each other's business coach.

People spend a lot of money to hire a coach, but you don't necessarily have to if you look through your contacts and find the perfect person willing to go on this journey with you. Finding someone to co-coach is probably the most important part of the process. This is an on-going relationship that will build from year to year. You definitely want to enjoy each other's company and respect what the other person has to say. Your coach should also inspire you and the two of you should want to gain knowledge from each other. Most of all, it should not affect your friendship. This needs to be an equal coaching partnership or it just won't work properly. Look through the names in your influential circle and see who fits the bill for you!

We recognized that we were the right match for each other and we could do this without outside help. We were both entrepreneurs, each had a strong business and marketing sense, and although we support each other, we don't compete. We're in completely different industries and our goal is to help each other succeed, not to be better than the other. We also inspire each other and can offer observations or comments without being judgmental. We're there to help, but it's still the other person's business.

We decided we'd kick out the old year and kick off the new with a set of plans and a commitment to help each other achieve them. The daily countdown phone calls began: twenty-nine days to the New Year, fifteen days to the New Year, and so on, until, finally, 2008 was behind us!

We met on January 1, 2009 for a champagne brunch to toast to a fabulous year. While everyone else was watching football and nursing hangovers, we were hard at work, sharing our business, financial, and personal goals, along with areas where we needed some help. We also spent part of the four-hour session brainstorming ways to improve our businesses. We were off!

That first year, we met once a month for lunch to review what we'd accomplished, what we wanted to achieve before the next session, and discussed any issues we had. In between meetings, we called each other once or twice a week for pep talks or quick updates, asking those time-honored words, "Are you being productive?" "What are you doing today that's making a difference in your business?" "Is there anything I can do to help?" "What do you need to do to move forward?"

By mid-year, we were both so busy we barely had time to chat!

We were convinced that our mutual support paid off. During our meetings and phone calls, we could freely discuss ideas, which prompted us to think them through more fully. We also created a safe environment in which to give constructive feedback to each other. Sometimes you don't recognize behavioral patterns, but someone else can! This has helped both of us change and strengthen our business backbones.

Though we achieved several goals, new opportunities arose—as often happens—and we took advantage of those which benefitted our companies. We also discovered that our goal-tracking methods helped us to make better decisions.

It wasn't all unicorns and rose-colored glasses. We had to learn to trust each other and understand how the other person thinks and works. We face different situations in our personal lives and have two completely different types of businesses. Through a lot of patience, listening, and commitment to helping each other be the best we could be, we've developed something greater than the sum of the parts.

Needless to say, when 2010 rolled around, we already had our goals laid out and we were ready to leap ahead into another successful year. Halfway through 2010, we already knew many of our goals for 2011. We're now better at looking at the bigger picture of where we each want to take our companies. Nowadays, we can actually visualize where we want to be in two to five years. It's a habit, a joy, to plan and track goals for our businesses. It's a lot of work, but it's definitely more fun when you have a safe environment to share and someone who believes in what you have to offer.

Our communication process has changed as well. We used to speak once or twice a week, but now it's almost daily. When you work alone, you can't have water cooler chats, but we make our own on the phone whenever we need a break.

We also have a greater understanding of our personal capabilities. When someone helps you think through the process, you can get further ahead than if you analyze it to death on your own.

If you'd like to pair up with a friend of yours to help each other achieve success, here are some suggestions:

Choose the right person. Try to find someone in a different field than your own. Remember, this is a support system, not a competition. Certainly, there's someone in your network who is strong in your weaknesses and vice versa. That way, you can glean something from each other's strengths. Make sure it's someone with whom you share a mutual respect. It won't work if it's a one-sided situation.

Build a strong bond. Even if you've known each other for awhile, going through this process is an adjustment. You'll learn different quirks and idiosyncrasies about each other and his/her work habits. Give it time. It truly took us that whole first year to get to that point.

Don't share secrets. Keep everything the two of you share completely confidential. Even if you have an opportunity or a contact for your coach, check with your coach first. Nothing should go beyond your conversations to anyone, not even to spouses or significant others. That includes brainstorming, challenges, opinions, connections, and so on.

Venting is good. Sometimes, you just need to do it. We'll call each other on occasion and say we just need to vent, and then we do. It's over, done with, and life goes on. Entrepreneurs sometimes need to have an outlet with someone who understands how hard it is to run a business.

Ask for a pep talk. Occasionally, you might have a down day. Or you could be going to an important meeting and you just aren't up to your best. Call your coach and ask for a pep talk. It works wonders!

Celebrate the little victories. Don't get caught up in the moment; look at how far you've come. Oftentimes, having that extra set of eyes on our business keeps us focused on moving forward, instead of wallowing in the present-moment mire. Every drop creates a wave. Remind yourself of what you've accomplished instead of dwelling and dreading the remaining to-do's on your list.

Skills are transferable. It's truly amazing how skills and information from one industry can be adapted to another. If you and your coach are in completely different industries, don't be afraid to share.

Track your progress. Use whatever method works for you. Just make sure you do it. By checking your progress against your goals, you're making decisions as to priorities, opportunities, and end results. These are a few different ways we've kept track:

Put everything in one notebook: goals, notes to yourself, accomplishments, opportunities, contacts, random thoughts. Whatever relates to your business, keep it all together.

Track it online I. List your goals in a Word document and number each one. Then create a separate sheet that's numbered to match your goals, and identify where you're going to spend your time that week. After awhile, you can look at all those weekly activity sheets and determine if you're spending your time in the right places.

Track it online II. Put it in Excel. You can list your goals, completion date, progress, and comments easily in a spreadsheet. Then you can put multiple years into one workbook and track your progress from year to year.

Track your finances, too. Most business owners have some sort of accounting software or use a bookkeeper, but you'd be surprised how many don't. Even if you do, having a spreadsheet with goals such as income streams, stretch revenue goals, percentage of total business, and others on one spreadsheet makes it quick and easy to discern exactly how you're doing. Once again, you can put multiple spreadsheets into one workbook and track from year to year.

Be patient. Wonderful things take time to build. Detours and challenges happen. It's called life. Many small businesses fail because people lack the patience to work through the rough times. Sometimes a detour will create something totally different than you had in mind, but it's okay if it's true to the business and the end result.

Take risks. No one ever got anywhere staying within his or her comfort zone. Many times, when we push ourselves outside of our comfort zones, great results occur.

Have fun! Business isn't always serious. The things from which we find the greatest rewards are relationships and discovering new opportunities, challenges, and edges to our comfort zones. If you enjoy what you're doing, you're going to be more productive and have greater rewards and success.

About the Authors

You don't have to be a celebrity to have your own stylist. Jenna Doughton is a personal style consultant, providing professional wardrobe advice to men and women around the country. She specializes in developing individual style. For over sixteen years, she has helped hundreds of women find their inner diva and express themselves through their wardrobes. She has assisted several companies in group settings and one-on-one with their employees, creating a professional environment that reflects the individual and company values at the same time.

Jenna Doughton may be contacted via:
www.jennadoughton.com
jenna@jennadoughton.com
Jenna, Inc.
(702) 569-1008

Cindi Maciolek is a writer and business consultant, helping small to mid-size companies with everything from strategic planning to marketing activities. Her book, *Divatiel: Reflections of a Bird's Companion,* is a true labor of love. *Java Jems: 5 Minute Inspirations for Busy People* is both a book and CD. She has also written for *Luxury Las Vegas* and *Robb Report* magazine. There's more to come. Stay tuned.

Cindi Maciolek may be contacted via:
cindi@cindimaciolek.com
www.twitter.com/cindimaciolek
www.facebook.com/pages/Cindi-Maciolek-Writer/185676404778438
(702) 341-5395

It's About Time

SANDY KASTEL

As I prepare for my show to announce the official release of my new album and my single "Indiana Rain" gains momentum on the radio, I think about the choices I've made and the steps I've taken toward my goals since the spring of 2001.

My husband, Harold, now retired, was the owner of the largest Winnebago/Itasca RV dealership in the United States. Six foot two inches tall, he is distinguished looking, his brown hair sprinkled with grey around the temples. His is a rags-to-riches story, a local farm boy who made it big. My sister arranged for me to meet Harold for lunch February 23rd, 1995. I had been working as a model and actress in commercials, film and TV, teaching a movement class to theater undergrad students at UNLV and performing with my own band around Las Vegas at hotels and corporate events. We hit it off right away. He proposed to me on his birthday in April and three years later it was official. We were man and wife.

May 17, 2001 (Seven Years Later)
Whiteland, Indiana

Our home on the south side of Indianapolis was in the city of Whiteland in a rural farm community, sprinkled with new custom homes and private estates residing alongside farmlands freshly graded and planted with corn, soy beans, and small family gardens. Nestled at the end of a long circular driveway was a formal rose garden at the entrance to a sprawling ranch style home on fifteen acres covered in white rock affectionately referred to as "Alabama hunk-n-chunk."

Harold and I were walking across the blacktop from the house to his race shop.

I stopped suddenly and turned to face him.

"What do you mean, 'No, you can't go?'"

Harold removed the toothpick from his mouth, tossed it to the ground and took a step backward.

"I don't want you to leave right now. Don't you want to go to the races with me?"

To the east of our home stood a rectangular building that looked like an oversized garage with wood side paneling and white stone matching the home. Three statuesque white pines, forty feet tall, guarded the structure. Four garage doors were wide open, revealing a collection of race cars, machines not commonly found in any barn or tool shed on a farm.

Attached to the back of the home was a large wood deck with carriage lights and a white country-style gazebo set away from the house and violet colored morning glory vines weaving through decorative trellises frame Victorian arches and doorways. Shading a European-carved stone picnic table is a twisted old oak tree missing a branch, the victim of lightning from the latest storm. Scattered throughout the property are groupings of maple trees, blue spruces, poplar trees, white pines, crabapples, and colorful flowerbeds.

Accustomed to a schedule full of dance classes, rehearsals and meetings, our Indiana home was at first a retreat where I often found myself sitting in the gazebo, reflecting on my life, spending hours playing the piano and writing songs, hoping to one day sing on stage again in my own show.

I discovered early in our relationship that being married was full of compromise and finding ways to balance my own career as a singer turned out to be even more challenging than I ever imagined.

In fact, every few years we were moving into a new and bigger home in Las Vegas and it was my responsibility to handle the move, the re-design and the decorating. On every move day Harold would say to me, "I'll see you tonight." And off he would go to the poker room at the Mirage or the golf course, leaving the old home and returning to the new one.

By the time we decided to remodel the 1980's ranch home my husband built in Indiana with his ex-wife, we had already moved four times. Even though it was a great experience to start from scratch and create a totally new environment for us, it was also a huge project. When the movers finally left that evening, before Harold arrived home from his dealership, the first thing I did was sit down at the Mason Hamlin grand piano in the middle of the newly decorated living room and begin to play.

Seven years and six homes later, I realized Harold's and my expectations of being married were a little different. I thought Harold would share my life and encourage my career as a singer and by now I had discovered he thought I would be content to be his wife and give up my dreams.

I admit, I enjoyed our lifestyle of traveling around the country to the races, owning homes in two totally different environments, designing and decorating them, planning parties and entertaining guests. It was also great to meet all the people involved with Harold's racing team, dealership and his large family. Along with the fun, though, there was also a lot of responsibility because of maintaining more than one residence.

Don't get me wrong. I'm not ungrateful. It's just that I'm a singer, always have been, always will be. There is a big part of me that loves to be on stage performing for an audience. I grew up in the *entertainment capital of the world* and my parents both had parts in my development as a performer. My father is a jazz musician. We started each day with him rehearsing in the living room. My mother sang and danced with her sisters when she was a young girl. She's the one who took me to my first audition, helped me learn my lines and sewed sequins and beads on my gowns for the pageants in which I competed. My whole life revolved around music and performing in one way or another. Now, for the first time, there was very little of it in my life.

When I met Harold he told me I would have to put "my music" on hold for a few years until we got married. Well, I did. When I was ready to go back to it full time, he wasn't. So this was the seventh year. I had spent the past four years trying to figure out how to incorporate my career with Harold's lifestyle. In 2001, I realized I was missing something in my life. Though I was happy to do all that was expected of me as a wife, my music had taken a back seat to my husband's business and our obligations as a couple due to the nature of owning an RV business and a race team.

We had been back at our Indiana home for a few weeks that summer when I discovered there was a music conference being held in Las Vegas. I wanted to attend. The keynote speakers were Chaka Khan and Mick Fleetwood.

"I really want to go to this conference." I said. *"It's been a long time since I did anything for my music."*

Harold has the mind of a businessman and really didn't understand why it was still important for me to continue to pursue my music now that I was married.

A race car, like a space shuttle or any other high-powered machine, is put through rigorous testing and re-testing, taken apart and put back together again; oiled and lubricated; tightened and tuned; so that finally, it has been polished and buffed to a high gloss sheen. The decals and logos are strategically placed for high visibility and maximum exposure. If the drivers do their jobs, win races, do what it takes to get ink, the cameras will zero in on them each time they fly down the track and the sponsors will be happy.

When we first met, Harold said he understood my passion for singing. He was passionate about drag racing, just like his team of racers. I thought he also understood that as a performer, my "vehicle" was my body and just like any race car, needed to be tuned-up on a regular basis in order to operate like a "fine running machine". Well, by now, my vehicle was feeling a little rusty, not quite up to speed and in dire need of a tune-up.

As I stood there watching Harold, I could see his focus was split between the race shop and me and without taking his eyes off the cars he said, *"Well, I don't want you to be away from me for that long."*

As I stood there facing Harold, I shrugged my shoulders and raised my hands to the sky. *"Do you realize we haven't been apart at all for almost seven years?"*

Turning to face me, he folded his arms across his chest and pouted. *"What does that have to do with anything? I don't want to be alone and I don't like eating by myself."*

On the fifteen-acre property I was surrounded by clues to my husband's lifestyle before we met. His second wife competed in shows with her Paso Fino horses. He had provided the necessary tools to support her passion of riding horses. There was a well-planned horse corral creating an inner perimeter for the horse's safety, a fence surrounding the lean-to, a pole barn, and feeding trough providing for shade in the summer and shelter in the winter, all necessary elements for even a small horse ranch.

In the middle of the property, where the grass is wilder and taller, there was also a lake, serene and almost hidden by the overgrowth of the aquatic plant life. A partially broken-down dock weathered from too much rain and too many years of neglect was in the beginning stages of repair. A fishing pole rested next to a plaid shirt; a bucket was filled with old rags and leather gloves; a hammer and a box of nails sat on top of a stack of freshly cut two by fours, tools waiting for something to do.

Leaning over the lake like a mother over a newborn child, a weeping willow waved her branches, gently skimming the water, creating ripples in the mirror's reflection, distorting the image of herself as the transplanted bluegill surfaced for air to nibble at her tender leaves; the faint bittersweet taste of the tears her lover weeps.

Turning to face Harold as he gazed across the lake, I placed my hands on his arms and tried to sooth his wounded ego.

"Honey, it's only for three days. You'll survive. Besides, you'll be with the guys at the races this weekend. You'll be having fun with them and I'll be back on Monday."

Left alone during the day while my husband went off to work, my days had become as abstract as Picasso's paintings, I moved from one role to another, going from wife, lover and hostess to singer, songwriter and performer. My life, like the vast landscape surrounding me had begun to take on a life of its own, crowding in on me.

One day a week earlier as I was strolling along the edges of the property under the grey skies, inhaling the pungent aromas of the underbrush and contemplating what to do, my legs became heavier and invisible spores riding on the damp air floated into my lungs, causing me to gasp. I realized my life was going around in circles, like the grassy path trimmed short by the bush-hog and wedged between the fence and row of trees of various shapes and sizes. This trail runs ten feet wide along the sides and around the back of the property. It is a place where one hears whispers and echoes of small creatures crunching over and under dead leaves, a reminder of the subconscious longings of my mind, slithering and sliding too close for comfort.

I wasn't sure what was bothering me, only that it felt as if I were caught up in a frenzy, like the crowds in a small town on the fourth of July watching a parade passing by on Main Street, my footsteps twisted and tangled, swallowed up in the confusion, not knowing which way to turn until I realized the sounds I was running from were only coming from inside my mind.

Being married to my husband had changed my approach to having a career in music. I wasn't available when the agencies called me for commercials, TV or film projects and because of Harold's travel schedule, it was no longer possible to be in shows running for months at a time. I had been trying to find a way to balance my career with our lifestyle. By taking this step, going to the music conference and getting feedback about the songs I was writing, I felt I had finally figured out a way to do it.

As I headed back to the house, I saw him standing there with his arms folded. It was a few minutes before he released them and wrapped them around me.

"All right. But you'd better be home by Monday or else."

I reached up and gave him a kiss,

The engines started inside the building and the noise became a roar. I rushed inside to the workbench, reached for the heavy-duty protective headphones in the cabinet above and put them on to protect my ears before I walked back outside. I knew I was on my own. The men were in their own world as they began loading the cars one by one. I had a lot to do to get ready and I rushed back to the house. Reaching for the screen door I turned and took one last look at the peaceful setting and wondered if it was the right choice.

The hickory trees, thick as thieves, were standing guard at the back of the property; the sentinels, tall and majestic, stoic and dense, were daring anyone to try and pass through them. There was no telling what I would find when I ventured beyond the woods at the edge of the line, for there is really no way of knowing where one road ends and the other begins when listening to our hearts and following our dreams.

"This will be good for me." I said to myself as the door closed behind me.

The first car they pulled out of the shop was a Super Comp Dragster. They rolled it onto the lift, pushed a button to raise it, then drove a red '67 Chevy II Bracket Car into the trailer and were on their way. As one Winnebago drove away with a trailer fully loaded, the next one pulled up in front of the race shop and they loaded a Comp-Eliminator Pontiac Trans Am and Super Stocker '68 Camaro, ready to go to the races.

Stout's Racing Team headed to the Indianapolis Raceway Park with four race cars for a chance to win thousands of dollars in cash and prizes as I packed a bag to board a plane headed back to Las Vegas and the chance to reconnect to my music.

May 21, 2001 (Four days later)

Harold and I were sitting on the deck in the backyard eating lunch. It was sunny and a breeze was flowing through the chimes. Hummingbirds were drinking from the feeders and a bluebird was grooming himself in our birdbath.

Harold was reading the newspaper while I was jotting down ideas in my notebook, eager to share everything about the weekend with him.

"And then I sang my song for him. He said it was really good because it could be recorded in different genres."

Harold nodded his head and I noticed the bird stretching his head around to reach the feathers on his left wing, which triggered something else I wanted to tell him.

"He said I'm a good lyricist because I paint pictures with my descriptions and I should write with other songwriters as much as possible, so I can get my songs out there."

Grinning, Harold reached out and took my hand in his.

"Sandy, I love you; and even though I don't always understand you, I finally realize I have to accept you the way you are."

"Really?" I asked, then smiled and said, *"It's about time."*

Present Day

Since that weekend ten years ago, I began focusing more on writing songs and visiting Nashville, Tennessee, on a regular basis, joined NSAI, the National Association of Songwriters International, attending their song camps, learning insights and tips from hit songwriters. I took the Pro Tools training to learn to use their software program so I could record demos of my songs. My husband sold his business and time spent at the drag races was limited to only a few weeks a year. The fifteen-acre ranch was traded for a home in Nashville and an opportunity for me to pursue my career as a recording artist and songwriter.

I attended writers' nights, meeting other songwriters with whom to co-write, hung out at the Bluebird Café, Tin Pan Alley, Music Row, and the Grand 'Ole Opry, listening to the music, learning as much as I could about songwriting and soaking up the energy that nurtures a songwriter's soul. It was like heaven every time I drove into the town that understood "it's all about the song."

My experiences with music growing up in Las Vegas had been different, from an entertainment point of view. This new outlook was inspiring to me and gave me an entirely new approach from which to look at my role in the music industry. Though both cities were built around music, one was built around entertainment and the other was built around the song. Nashville created an environment where audiences sit quietly in anticipation, listening to writers tell the "story behind the song" before singing an acoustic version of it. This varies dramatically from the lavish productions audiences expect to see when they come to Las Vegas.

Then in 2007, I released *This Time Around*, which was recorded in Nashville and Las Vegas, a tribute to the Great American Songbook and *Only in Las Vegas*, a collection of songs from my televised show. Two years before, I began working on my original album and my goal was to make it "all about the songs." I was fortunate to work with three wonderful producers on this album even though the process took longer than planned, working around everyone's schedules.

First, I worked with my producer, Ron Aniello, recording three of my original songs. Next, he got feedback from radio promoters, who all liked the same song and suggested we build the entire album around that song, which meant researching songs from other writers. Ron reached out to publishing houses and after listening to about a hundred songs; we narrowed it down to five.

My next step was to co-write two songs with the other producers, Jimmy Haslip and Jeff Lorber. Once this was done, we set a date to record the tracks in a Nashville studio and picked one more of my originals to add to the album.

Then my husband decided to build a new home back in Indiana. Once again, I had to divide my time between my music and my obligations as a wife. It was both exciting and challenging, my creative juices working overtime, ideas flowing back and forth between the two unrelated worlds. I was juggling again and it took delicate maneuvers to keep it all in balance. Just when I thought I had it all under control, another ball was thrown into my court and everything came crashing to a sudden halt.

The doctors discovered my mother had a cancerous tumor in her lung. I put a hold on everything in order to spend the time to find out what we had to do. After a month of tests and visits to various doctors, the decision was made to take her to UCLA for surgery. Once I was sure she was out of danger, I returned to finish my album.

The next spring all the recordings were finished, the mixing done, and the mastering completed. The lyrics, credits, and photos were gathered and sent to the graphics designer for the album packaging to be designed and sent on to the manufacturers for printing. With the album ready, there would be radio promoters, publicists, and marketing teams to put in place, all waiting for the signal to release the first single to radio.

Every year life teaches me something new. In 2001, it taught me to listen to my heart. It also taught me that no one else is going to hand me my dreams. It is up to me to figure out a way to make them part of my everyday life, rather than putting them on "hold" while life happens. By taking the step to "get reconnected to my music," I was able to accomplish my goals, one by one.

My message to anyone *pursuing your passion* is be sure to remember these *five* steps:

1. *Listen* to your heart. The passion for our dreams lies within our souls, waiting to become reality.

2. *Prepare* yourself to achieve your goals. Take the necessary steps. If you choose to be successful in life, continue to learn something about your craft every day.

3. *Be flexible*. Plans don't always turn out the way we expect. We may need to pause or stop along the way and re-assess what needs to be done.

4. *Stay focused*. Keep your eye on the target. Distractions may take your attention away from your ultimate desired result.

5. *Be open* to the possibilities. No matter how we try to anticipate the future, there is still no way to predict the outcome.

Most importantly, as you continue on life's fascinating journey, remember it is up to you, and you alone, to pursue your passion.

Excuse me, my cell phone is ringing now and it's playing my new favorite song *Indiana Rain*. This is the call I've been waiting for all year.

"Hello! It's about time."

About the Author

Sandy Kastel inspires others to believe in themselves, follow their dreams and create their own success. An extensive musical education in a variety of styles beginning at the age of four prepared her for a lifelong career in the entertainment industry.

Receiving accolades as a singer, Sandy won the Miss Nevada title and the talent award in the Miss America pageant which became a springboard for opportunities on stage, in film and television.

The owner of SKS Sights and Sounds, Inc., Sandy creates and produces corporate and private events, film documentaries, independent films and is in production on the Broadway-bound version of *The Notebook* by author Nicolas Sparks with composer Ron Aniello and songwriter Joy Bethany.

A recording artist and songwriter, Sandy has recorded three albums, owns her own label, Silk and Satin Records, and is developing young artists. Sandy's songs are licensed for commercials, television and film around the world.

Sandy is a second time author in the *Life Choices* series. She is a highly sought after performer, speaker, personal coach and is available for concerts, corporate events, seminars and workshops.

Sandy Kastel may be contacted via:
Turning Point International
Las Vegas, NV
(702) 896-2228
info@sandykastel.com
www.sandykastel.com
www.facebook.com/sandykastelmusic
www.twitter.com/sandykastel
www.linkedin.com/sandykastel

Put Yourself Last: A Reality Check

BILL LYNCH

After forty-two years in business, becoming an MBA, and having the opportunity to serve as a CEO of large and small companies, I have seen it all (well, almost.) I have experienced some of the greatest successes and failures, some of the strongest profits and nauseating losses, both sides of almost every coin. So through and through, what drives my passion for business? What makes me tick? What fuels me? Truth. In business, there is conventional wisdom and reality. There is textbook knowledge and there is real life knowledge. At the end of the day, what delivers real sustainable results? What keeps business growing? I live and operate by this one truth and I am here to testify that it works.

Put yourself last. That's right. Selfless business creates strong profits. Operate within your value system. Put employees, suppliers, and customers before yourself. And always work with integrity.

VALUES

Conventional Wisdom: "It would be nice to do the right thing, but this is business. That morality stuff works at church and maybe at home, but you can't bring it to work. Profit and shareholder wealth rule business."

Reality: During my career, it made me twinge to hear statements such as those. When my boss used them, double twinge. If you have felt this way, know you are not alone. And yes, I have done things to keep a job that I really wished I had not done.

When I was just starting in business back in the late sixties, I was sent to a time management course. I don't remember who sponsored or taught it, but I still remember the core premise:

How you spend your time reflects not only your goals but also your values. Keep your activities within the playing field defined by your values and you will be happy and successful. Stray from your values and you will be miserable...no matter how much money you make.

When I became a CEO, our business plans started with the core values of the corporation. These included statements like:

We value the worth and dignity of every individual

We value integrity in all of our relationships with suppliers, employees, and customers.

We value operating from a moral-centered core.

You get the idea.

The board of directors found this out of place and hard to comprehend. One of the directors, who was fond of quoting Warren Buffett, agreed to keep our value statements in the plan, but made it clear we better focus on shareholder value at any cost. Another, a Stanford MBA, suggested "we value cash flow" made more sense to him. Pretty typical of what is wrong with us MBAs, I think.

Now realize that a lot of lip service is paid to values in organizations. I suspect the value statements in the Enron business plan did not say, "We value fooling everyone watching while we rack up big bonuses and stock profits." Actually the *New York Times* reported on Enron values: *"We treat others as we would like to be treated ourselves."* Fair enough. Enron elaborates: *"We do not tolerate abusive or disrespectful treatment. Ruthlessness, callousness, and arrogance don't belong here."* Looking from the outside, ruthlessness, callousness, and arrogance defined the senior management team. Value statements are useless unless they are activated every day in the way business is done.

EMPLOYEES

Conventional Wisdom: Pay market wages and be as frugal as humanly possible with benefits, work rules, and other forms of compensation. They are the workers; we are the owners, after all.

Reality: We consistently put employees first, not customers. Why? The employees create value for customers and turn them into happy, satisfied repeat customers. A honked-off employee never made a customer squeal with delight. Squeal? Maybe. A machine operator crying on the job never made an excellent product. Why was she crying? She left her seven-year-old at home sick because day care wouldn't take her and she was afraid to miss work and jeopardize her job.

At that company, our policies combined vacation and sick time and allowed employees to take as little as two hours at a time. No reason was necessary for the time off. Notice at least the day before was requested, but exceptions were certainly made. Was it convenient for management? No! What did it really cost us? Not very much compared to the pressures it took off working parents.

What happened if your mother died in another state and you couldn't afford to travel to the funeral? What if your ten-year-old car needs repair or you can't get to and from work? At our company, we worked out an arrangement with a local credit union to guarantee loans up to one week's pay for any employee, regardless of credit, with a twelve-month payment plan. Employees were allowed one loan at a time. Employees had to sign to allow payroll deduction including the balance owed at the time of termination for any reason. What did it cost us? We lost an occasional balance at termination…usually our own fault. We had to keep track of the program. Ultimately, not much compared to the employee loyalty, morale, and increased quality-of-life which our employees received.

If you have a parent-teacher conference scheduled for your child, we want you to go. Take personal time or take it without pay, but go. I know most MBAs will have a hard time with the concept, but sometimes there are things that really are more important than being at work.

Have you ever observed the "full day in four hours" phenomenon? That is the last day before a holiday weekend when the supervisor announces that if we can get our department scheduled work out by noon, everyone can go home for the remainder of the day with pay. It almost never fails to happen. That same phenomenon usually occurs among the other employees when one of their own needs to be away for a personal reason.

If you act this way, will some take advantage? Too seldom to worry about once people realize you genuinely care about them. Those who do will be pressured by their peers to conform. (At least that's the theory. I can't say from experience I have ever seen it happen. Some things are never okay to share with the boss.) Sometimes you have to fire someone. We love employees, but we don't call them family. You are stuck with family for life.

Every employee should have the right to shut down a line for safety or quality reasons. They may not always prevail, but they should be encouraged to take ownership of safety and quality issues. Usually we set our internal quality standards well within the acceptable customer specifications. Sometimes something may not meet our internal standards, but is still within the acceptable window for the customer. Prove that to the employee who raised the issue and work to get back within the internal limits. People want to be respected and valued. Show them; don't just put up posters.

Share your company goals with every employee and let them know how they are doing compared to the goal. Let everyone participate in the celebrations. Pizza and T-shirts don't cost much. With the right atmosphere and the right words, they mean a lot. Scale the rewards to the accomplishment. We recently hit a major target in our printing company and everyone in the company (except me) got an extra week's pay as a bonus. The employees organized a party for me complete with silly string and confetti. (Large pieces this time; it took six months to finally vacuum up from the last confetti celebration.) They learned about the bonus after the party.

SUPPLIERS

Conventional Wisdom: Negotiate their prices so they break even if you can, then pay them just before you need to order again and still take the cash discount. Complain about the quality and ask for discounts for defective products. Threaten to go elsewhere frequently.

Reality: These are usually the most abused stakeholders in any business. It is your suppliers who provide the materials that allow you to satisfy your customers. Besides, they are human beings who deserve to be treated with respect and integrity. We negotiate once a year. After that, we don't bring up cost until the next year. We will go into our line of credit to ensure that our suppliers are paid on time, as agreed. We stick with one supplier in each category, preferring to have a partner rather than managing a constant price comparison through bidding.

Our refrigerator is always open to the UPS guy and other vendor delivery people who come to our plant regularly. Our folks had a birthday party for one of the regulars who drops off supplies almost every day at the plant. Our bindery equipment salesman just left to go with a national equipment supplier. He brought his boss by on his final visit and announced we were the best customer he had. We make baseball and hockey tickets available to our most important vendors just like we do for our customers.

How much more does it cost us? I'm sure we leave a few percentage points on price up front on some things. On the other hand, when paper supplies are short, we get a call telling us what we need to order to be protected. When a piece of equipment needs emergency service, we have the cell phone number of the repairman. (He is forbidden from giving it out by his company.) In a big business card fiasco, one of our suppliers gave us credit for his whole contribution to the project. Supplier goodwill and a partnering relationship pay dividends in customer service and customer satisfaction.

CUSTOMERS

Conventional Wisdom: Every dollar you spend beyond just what it takes to satisfy a customer is wasted. It should go to the shareholders instead.

Reality: Sorry, but customers who are just satisfied customers are more price sensitive and more prone to change suppliers than those who are excited to do business with you.

Carrie Wilkerson, a million dollar a year speaker/entrepreneur recently said from the platform: "Honey, my customers don't love me. They love the fact that I love them." This is our customer service philosophy. Love them and they will know that you do.

Our largest printing customer has more than fifty branches and a somewhat confusing internal order processing system. We often catch that a branch has just ordered something we already shipped yesterday. We gave that customer a small price increase last year and their response: we don't buy from you because of price; we buy because you have our backs.

INTEGRITY

Conventional Wisdom: A lie is as good as the truth if the customer or the supplier buys it. Our loyalty is to shareholder wealth, nothing else.

Reality: We have only one customer satisfaction policy: the customer is always right. If the customer is not happy, we will fix it. If we can't fix it, we don't want to be paid for it.

A recent case: a new customer ordered eight sets of business cards for senior staff. We printed them and delivered them. The CEO saw them for the first time and hated them. They had been ordered by the COO and were exactly what she ordered. The CEO did not like the way the cards were designed. We agreed to remake them at our cost. Subsequently, the CEO wanted to completely redesign the cards and change the stock. We did that with no extra charge. We delivered exact samples on the new stock and had both approve them. We delivered the new cards and they both hated them. The stock was not what they approved. "This stuff is as thin as toilet paper," the CEO explained. Our salesperson was in tears. In spite of the fact that the approved samples and the delivered cards were the exact same thickness, according to our measurements with a digital micrometer, we picked them up and credited back the invoice. The COO yelled they would never use us again. Thank God.

Integrity goes beyond being honest. It goes to standing behind every aspect of the work of your business. Employees see the way you deal with customers.

This is a book about passions. Be passionate about doing things well. Be passionate about doing the right things. Don't listen to those who tell you the way to success is to wring every nickel twice to increase shareholder value at the expense of your integrity, your values, and your moral center.

I can testify that putting yourself last is a great strategy for success... if you define success as I do: being extraordinarily happy with your lot in life.

About the Author

Bill Lynch, president of Comsel Communication, writes, consults and speaks on customer acquisition and revenue growth for small to mid-sized businesses. Lynch shares his recipe for success in helping small business owners develop business plans, deal with the financial realities of small business, and clarify the roles of cold calling and networking. He assists small business owners in understanding the value of a new customer and how much to invest to acquire one. Lynch teaches people the need to trust yourself to produce high value results and offers solutions on how to do so.

Lynch bought a failing Minuteman Press franchise in 2005 averaging $5,000 a month in sales and turned it into a million dollar business. Prior to his franchise purchase, Lynch was President and CEO of a $20 million company manufacturing and importing cleaning products for major retailers and janitor supply distributors.

Lynch spent over 40 years in sales, marketing and senior management positions. He has an MBA from the University of Chicago Booth School of business.

He is an Affiliate member of the North Texas Chapter of the National Speakers Association. His articles appear regularly in www.BusinessNorthTexas.com, the SCORE newsletter and other business publications. His blog on Networking has developed a loyal following.

Bill Lynch may be contacted via:
www.ComselCommunication.com
Bill@comselcommunication.com

Lessons Learned in the Dirt

KEVIN B. PARSONS

"This is madness," I muttered into my helmet. I raced down a dirt road, going ninety-plus miles per hour, and at fifty-three years of age found myself competing with people thirty years younger. The bike and I roared through the desert, a rooster tail of dust in our wake. The 520 mile race, 'Vegas to Reno,' is the longest off-road race in the United States. It's a marathon of rocky washes, dusty trails, and deep silt similar to riding through powdered sugar. Bob, age forty, started at daybreak and handed the bike to Roger, age forty-six, at pit two. At mile 110, I took over.

I could see a right turn ahead and slowed considerably. I gingerly negotiated the curve, then shifted up through the gears, once again into the nineties. This smooth segment helped matters considerably, allowing me some respite. The tight, rocky sections with their jarring and harsh bumps hurt the worst. After forty-five miles, I zipped along, five miles from the short-term goal, the pit stop at mile 165, where I could hand the bike off to Bob. He could take over the racing again, giving me a well-deserved rest. Surviving the heat and dust, I also endured a great deal of pain.

I was riding with a broken collarbone.

Forty miles previously, I took a trip over the handlebars as the front wheel dug into some silt at fifty miles per hour and catapulted me to the ground.

Motorcycles and racing have been my passion from age thirteen. I saved my money, bought a bike, and fixed it up to race. I usually finished mid-pack, but the racing bug stung me, and good. Sitting at the starting line with bikes on either side, waiting for the starter to throw the flag, the adrenaline provided a natural high that even four decades later, still charges the batteries like nothing else. The searing pain in my shoulder, along with the inability to hold onto the bike with my left hand lessened the enthusiasm.

I pulled into the pit and handed the bike to Bob. Roger helped me remove my protective gear and shirt. Sure enough, the bone pressed against my skin like a broken pencil behind a sheet. As the team loaded the truck to leapfrog to another pit, I stopped by the paramedic and got a sling. I rode along in the chase truck for the next 355 miles, or nine hours. No time for emergency rooms. I knew from experience that a few days made no difference.

We soldiered on, Roger and Bob taking turns on the bike, and I rode in the pit truck, offering nothing more than encouragement. However, sticking with the team and cheering them on provided motivation for everyone. At 450 miles, Roger took his turn flying over the bars. Nothing broken, but he limped into the pit and handed the bike to Bob, the last rider and the only one in any shape to continue. The pit crew attached the headlight as the sun dipped below the Sierras.

Sixteen hours after the start, Bob brought the bike to the finish, riding under the checkered flag as portable light towers illuminated our joy. Finishing 'Vegas to Reno' always gives me the greatest feeling of accomplishment. And 'Ding! Ding!' Bonus. We won our class. Broken, filthy, and exhausted, we grinned like idiots.

'Vegas to Reno' occurred halfway through the 'Best in the Desert' racing season. We struggled with more than injuries. At the Laughlin season opener, we suffered three flat tires and finished as one of the last overall competitors. Leading the race in Parker, our engine broke after two-thirds of the race and we DNF'd (Did Not Finish). For championship points, the team could drop a race, so we tossed Parker. After only two races we had already used our mulligan.

We managed the Terrible's 250 in Pahrump without incident. The team ran steadily all day long, and finished strong, winning our class.

The Las Vegas 150 in Jean threw us a curve ball. Before the race started, the skies opened and torrents of rain fell on the desert. The dry lake bed, established for pitting, now swallowed tents, bikes, and gear in water. Injured and unable to race, I drove the chase truck to provide the next rider, fuel, and tools for the team. The Bureau of Land Management ticketed us for speeding, so we missed Roger at the first pit. We rushed to the second, hoping to beat him. With moments to spare we refueled the bike and the other rider took over. We finished that race after much chaos and confusion.

The season ending Henderson 400 at the Eldorado dry lake bed proved to be a survival run. Roger and I healed enough to race and we managed to keep upright and finish that day.

We made an incredible amount of mistakes that season. Each mistake gave us lessons for being better competitors in off-road racing, and in life, too.

At Laughlin, we raced a new bike and saw it limp into the pits three times with flat tires. While a fresh ride sounds like a great idea, we failed to install thicker inner tubes to prevent flat tires. How about the Las Vegas 150 and the rain? We failed to prepare for unexpected events. Rain gear, heavier gloves, and spare goggles (not to mention a headlight) would have given us a competitive edge. Inferior equipment caused Parker to be our DNF race. We left the stock chain guide instead of installing a $30 racing one, so the chain flew off and broke the engine cases, a $1,700 fix, with valuable points lost. What do these lessons teach us in life? Watch the little things. They can trip you up. Prepare. You can't go into a business meeting or make a presentation without being adequately prepared. Proper preparation prevents pathetic, poor performance.

What about my collarbone? I trained less than Roger and Bob, and raced a motorcycle unfamiliar to me. I rode above my abilities. The life lesson? Train and don't overreach. Know your limits and stay within them. Pace yourself.

The largest challenges that season loomed behind us. Racing off-road requires nerves of steel as the rider roars along a wash, watching for that rock which could end his race. However, nothing instills fear in a dirt biker more than a 750 horsepower trophy truck roaring up and passing, burying the rider in dust. "Please, dear God, let there not be another one trying to pass now," remains a fervent prayer of the racer. These mammoth pickups start their race three hours behind the bikes, but with a top speed of over 140 miles per hour, can catch over one-third of the field before the race is over. Yet when the trucks caught us, we continued struggling to hear, over the roar of our own engine, the trophy truck early enough to get safely out of the way.

Amazingly, we won the championship in our class. Who would have thought that a team, making that many mistakes—big ones—could win a championship? To what could we give the credit? We refused to allow obstacles to stop us. Flat tires? Fix them and keep going. Rain? Race in the dark, struggle to see through the downpour. Broken collarbone? Pick up the bike, get on and race with one arm until you get to the next pit stop. We maintained team integrity, prepared and entered every race, and did everything we could to finish, no matter what. The three of us kept focused through the season, encouraging one another in spite of our mistakes. Roger, Bob, and I went the distance.

Let's review the lessons:

1. Watch the little things and be prepared.
2. Train and pace yourself.
3. Don't allow obstacles to keep you from going the distance.
4. Face your fears.

What's your passion and what are its challenges? Business? You must overcome a myriad of obstacles. I haven't spoken to an entrepreneur who said, "I never imagined it being that easy." Employee challenges, regulations, competitors, and market forces all assault you, challenging you to DNF. Yet the business owner shrugs on a backpack, assembles his gear, and fights the good fight. When the business succeeds, the victory is that much sweeter. No matter what your passion or challenge, the race is long, yet the reward is great. I often say, "The best things in life are hard."

Is family your passion? To train your children to be responsible adults? The obstacles may be the school, extended or blended family, their peer group, or even the children themselves. This race is a long one, a minimum of eighteen years. Yet the parent must get up, look in the mirror, face his fears and say, "I'm going to be a great leader for my child." Nevertheless, the reward at the end of a long race is worth it.

For us, we won the championship series. The team received twenty dollar trophies, really tacky sweatshirts, and cheap key rings. However, the recognition at the awards banquet and the knowledge that we finished on top made all the pain and struggle worth it. At the beginning of the season, we never anticipated having so many obstacles to overcome. Nor did we imagine winning the championship. Watching our bike come in with the third flat tire in the opening race, so far back, we couldn't in our wildest dreams visualize hoisting our trophies at the post-season banquet. A shiny gold "1" hangs on the key to my car, which reminds me of our great accomplishment every time I use it.

Do you have a passion that really makes you come alive? Just because you have a passion doesn't mean you'll automatically excel at it. Chances are, you will. Why have a passion that only generates mediocrity? Certainly you must work at it, tweak and polish it until you really shine. When it finally clicks, reaches critical mass, or operates on all cylinders, however you describe it, that is when the passion fulfills you and makes you come alive, being all that God created you to be.

What is your passion? What do you love to do? Do you love your job? Is there something you would like to do well? What is your dream? What are you doing about that dream? The great philosopher, Erma Bombeck (okay, she was a humorist) said, "There are people who put their dreams in a little box and say, 'Yes, I've got dreams, of course I've got dreams.' Then they put the box away and bring it out once in awhile to look in it, and yep, their dreams are still there."

It's time to kick your fears to the curb, get those dreams out of the box, and pursue them. They could take you to places you never imagined.

About the Author

Kevin grew up Seattle, Washington, and rather than have an affair, moved to Las Vegas for a mid-life crisis. He's written *Ken Johnson & Roxi the Rocker*, an illustrated children's book. His story, *My Love Misplaced*, was published in *Seeking God First*, an anthology. The teaser for his novel, *Silent Night, Holy War*, first of a three book series, is published in *Writer's Bloc III*, an anthology.

Along with writing and speaking, Kevin owns five businesses in the construction and real estate industries. He's a member of Toastmasters, Henderson Writers Group, and American Christian Fiction Writers.

Kevin rides and races motorcycles for fun. One goal is to ride a motorcycle at 200 mph. He's been close; 194 at El Mirage dry lake bed in California.

Kevin is blessed with four children and six grandchildren. He resides in Las Vegas with his patient wife, Sherri, and their dog Max, who is an idiot.

Kevin Barry Parsons may be contacted via:
710 W. Sunset Rd., #110
Henderson, NV 89011
(702) 429-4866
kparsons901@aol.com
www.kevinbparsons.com

$\mathscr{S}$trength

A great leader's courage to fulfill his vision comes from passion, not position.

—*John Maxwell*

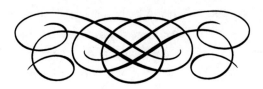

A Place I've Never Been

DELORES RAMSEY MCLAUGHLIN

Lying in bed, I felt a bit of uneasiness. My heart beat in quick thuds, and there was swelling inside that immobilized me. I had no way out. I realized I must have been having a terrible panic attack. It was 3:00 a.m., Sunday morning, and he was not home yet. No call. Nothing. My mind wandered to the things that could have happened to him. He might be lying in the ditch, hurt, with no one to help him. But I knew there were other explanations that were matters of his own choosing, and they were just as likely to provide an explanation, and I feared them even more. The rage of terror was growing each minute as I lay there and thought about it. Looking at the clock, it was now 3:30 a.m. The hands on the clock seemed to be taking their time. I felt such pain and emptiness. Most of all, I felt helpless. I knew I couldn't just lie there, letting fate or the will of this man, or perhaps both, control me. I needed to do something. Calling the police might be useless. Rolling over to the side of the bed, I quickly jumped up, as if I had been administered electric shock treatment. The tears were pouring down my face. My body felt played out and useless. With the last of whatever strength was left in me, I thought, "I can't take any more of this. I've got to pull myself together. He's a grown man and he knows what he's doing." I cried aloud. I went to the bathroom and began to wash my face. In the mirror, a woman with a thin face, red puffy eyes, a faraway lost aspect looked back at me. I had no idea what I was going to do, but I had to do something.

Dressed and ready to go, I called my sister, Candace. She answered the phone. I asked her to come over and go with me.

"Where are we going?" she asked.

"I don't know, but please go with me," I begged her.

Candace arrived at 7:15 a.m. I took careful note of the time, even as my world was falling apart. Candace looked at me with a puzzled expression and said, "Did he come home last night?" This was not the first time she had been asked to provide the support system for gathering strength against the chaos this man had caused.

In a shaky voice, I replied, "No." I was tired of being treated this way. I couldn't handle too much more of this.

"Where are you taking us?" Candace asked again. I told her I didn't know where I was going, but I had this feeling that I would find him that morning. I remembered him talking about the group's motor home and it being in a trailer park, out on the east side of town, close to Van Buren.

I parked the car alongside the road, and looked at Candace. "I want you to go with me," I said. As I got out of the car, I couldn't believe I had actually been led to a place where I had never been. Not knowing where I was going, I felt in my heart that direction would come. There, next to the motor home, was his car. The scene seemed unreal, a quality of chaos and betrayal permeating the whole of this otherwise unremarkable setting. Feeling an endless rage coming over me, I suddenly had no fear at all. I walked up to the trailer door, grabbed the knob, and to my surprise, it opened freely. No struggle. Just acceptance.

As I walked in, the silence was unbearable. The odor of familiar cologne enveloped me. As I stood in the doorway, I saw him lying there in the bed. Without a care in the world. The gentle, untroubled cadence of his breathing underscored the serenity of his mood. His nude body, with buttocks exposed, was in a posture of complete contentment. All that had seemed to me to be private to our world was there on display for anyone who cared to push open an unlocked trailer door. Next to him lay a woman with short cropped hair, echoing the same peaceful breathing pattern of his tranquil rest. She lay there wrapped freely in his arms, an invader in our private world of love. Standing within this setting that was to him peaceful and safe, my own world grew stone-like, cold and completely enveloped by a searing and inescapable pain.

I stood there frozen for what seemed like hours, though in real time, only a few moments passed by. The swelling inside me that before could not be moved came pouring out, and streamed down my face in the form of hot tears. I felt the power of speech begin to return. From the pit of my stomach and my soul, I screamed at him, and I could hear the loud, high-pitched cry that came from me. "Ben, how could you do this?" At the sound of my voice, he immediately jumped out of bed, his limbs moving in a startled manner, shaking with the quick, shifting actions of his body. At the sight of this man, naked in body and betrayal, I felt my own body change to battle mode. I felt the rage of the bull taunted by the red cape. He approached me. I extended both hands and pushed him away.

"Let me explain," he fumbled. "You know I love you and wouldn't do anything to hurt you." I looked up into his eyes and saw a hopeless, worthless, shallow character that could never understand the tragedy I was feeling.

I could hear my sister in the background saying, "You no good bastard! How could you do this to my sister? You no good piece of ..." She continued to speak, but I could no longer hear her words. It was the moment and the day I realized I was passionate for the passionless. Once upon a time there was love, and feelings and words mattered. What mattered now? Nothing. It was over.

When we see a story in the movies or on TV, or even when we encounter it in real life, we see somebody who has a run of amazingly good or bad fortune; "there but for the grace of God go I." The "No" comes in, however, when we get down to serious analysis of the question. Few people take it to that level for a variety of reasons; after all, we reason, "These really aren't situations we're ever going to have to face. It may happen in fiction or to the other guy, but it sure isn't going to happen to me." Indeed, the thought is so remote that it seems strange even to think about it. The good "What Ifs" wrap us in dreams that may distract us from everyday work, and the bad "What Ifs" are so frightening, we back away. Instead of pondering either seriously, we quickly sweep them from our minds and move on to less unsettling subjects. We all need to lead happier and more meaningful lives, as well as give ourselves a fascinating tour of what we are really about. A startling revelation comes into focus for all of us. That revelation is: few, if any of us are actually spending our time on this earth each day doing what we truly deem most important.

Understanding what is important to us promotes insight of our purpose and the ability to pursue it passionately. Sometimes, we can pursue someone or something that is not good for us and which can lead us to a place that can hinder our personal growth in life. Ben was a man whom I loved deeply and pursued him passionately. Furthermore, I desired to find Ben the night he did not come home and the passion within me would not let me stop until I did. As a result, I followed my passion of love for Ben which brought me discovery not only of his relationship with someone else, but self-discovery about myself. I realized I pursued the passion of Ben, neglecting my own passion and benefits. This self-discovery was noteworthy in my life and future successes because it allowed me to comprehend the true meaning of passion. In other words, when we truly want something so badly that our inner energy takes us to a level of supernatural awareness, the realization of successfully reaching our passion is great. This is a moment that we never expect, but when it happens there is an emotional surge. The message becomes loud and clear: "Follow your passion and not others."

Life misfortunes can change our lives. These experiences enlighten us to changes that will make an impact in our knowledge and awareness. My experience with Ben has taught me important information about pursuing my passion. First, a true pursuit of passion will lead us to a place we've never been. Secondly, there will be risk involved, which requires courage to proceed. Third, awareness of the direction to go will come at unforeseen times. Next, we must be willing to forgive self and others. Lastly, pursing our passion requires development of an openness to learn from the experience. For this reason, I am pursuing my passion wholeheartedly in communicating both nationally and internationally through speaking, teaching, preaching, singing, and writing. I hope to inspire others to pursue their dreams and not be intimidated by the process. Consequently, education, experience, and life situations have prepared me to empower others. I am thankful for the opportunity to share what I have learned. I finally understand what is truly important to me and can be a role model in pursuing a life of substance, sustainability, and balance mentally, physically, and spiritually. Interestingly, I have learned to be brave, pursue my passion freely, and with no regrets.

About the Author

Delores Ramsey McLaughlin is a motivational speaker who can inspire audiences from corporate to faith-based. She has a gift of making the most serious topics become less intimidating and more accepting. The founder and executive director of All Out Communication and Freedom-N-Christ Ministries, she teaches effective leadership skills, strategies to successfully pursue your dreams, and how to bridge gaps between cultural and religious differences. Delores' passion lies in communicating on all levels to maintain effective communication. She has a bachelor's degree in communication, a master's in leadership and is the senior minister of Freedom-N-Christ. She also enjoys professional membership with the National Speaker's Association.

Delores McLaughlin may be contacted via:
Post Box 8205
Phoenix, Arizona 85066
nthaeyezz@cox.net
(623) 203-1573

Passion is Your Reward for Connecting to Your Spirit

MARISA WOLLHEIM

"What you are is your Gift from God...
What you make of yourself, is your Gift to God!"

The very first time I read these words on a greeting card, it triggered something in me...and only many years later, my journey revealed and pointed out the depth of these words to me.

My journey started more than twenty years ago when my Gran, who was living with us, was diagnosed with cancer and the doctors gave her three months to live. We were devastated and overwhelmed with different feelings; fear and inadequacy often got the better of us. At the time, I was sixteen and being the only child, my Ouma* was my best friend. I took her illness very seriously. I became the observer, watching the adults in my life experience what I later learned to be first-hand grief.

Although stressful and sad, I know this truly was one of the most soulful times of my life! When my Ouma's dying process started, we had the blessing of having a dear friend, Jon—a nurse and psychic—come and stay to assist us. We saw that his blessed awareness of life after death and understanding of spiritual healing—as my parents were engaged in spiritualism and my father was a renowned healer—brought my Ouma comfort and relief.

One morning, Jon told my mom to call the family together as he could see my Ouma's spirit starting to leave her body and she was slipping into a coma. Throughout the day, Jon described the scene to us. He asked, "Who was this man with a moustache that did this and that? He is accompanied by so and so..." and I remember the surprised looks on my mom and her sister's faces as they recognized this to be my Ouma's brother. It was like a birthing or a coming home where everyone had come to prepare and welcome the weary traveler. At one point, he described that angelic-like beings had brought a stretcher covered in St. Joseph lilies for her to lie on, but she did not want to lie there as she was afraid of hurting or damaging the flowers. It took some convincing for her to realize that she did not have a material body that could damage the flowers.

As soon as all the family arrived, Jon manipulated a pressure point at the back of Ouma's neck and held her head up gently; she came to and was able to look at each one while giving her last greeting. She could not speak, yet one could sense what she wanted to say.

It had been a long day and night. My mom was drained, so Jon told her to go and lie down. Mom was afraid that my Ouma would die while she was not there and thus made Jon promise that he would call her. I went to lie down with my mom and after some time there was a loud knock on my mom's glass top dressing table, which made my mom and me sit up straight in bed, just when Jon walked in to call us.

My mom shared that before she lay down she asked God to please wake her before her mom passed, so the knock on the dressing table was a true sign—as it was at the far end of the room where no one had access to it. As a young person, that phenomena impressed me and contributed to me trusting the "process" much later in my life.

It was so real being in that room, absolutely present, waiting for that moment when Ouma's last breath was taken…Jon could see what is termed the 'golden cord' that attaches us to our spirit like the unseen umbilical cord. Then that last breath and silence…

We had witnessed the birthing process of a spirit gone home.

Jon encouraged the family to have coffee and leave the body during this sacred time to allow the spirit to release completely.

Five years later, one of our congregation members was admitted to a local hospice in Johannesburg and while visiting him, I was so inspired and touched by the work that I made it my goal to open a hospice on the West Rand. That is exactly what I did. Going on inspiration, a vision and many a rummage sale, I paid off a house and was now ready to make it available to the movement to start a hospice on the West Rand. I served on the steering committee as the secretary and before long I was running the hospice. This was the beginning of my journey of self-discovery and passion. Experience was my first teacher and the patients became my greatest teachers. Whatever I had learned in my life to that point—physically, mentally, emotionally, and especially spiritually, came forth as pearls of wisdom when I was sitting down with people facing their deepest moments of fear, peace, or anguish.

I attended hospice training, read books, and met Dr Elizabeth Kubler-Ross – from whom I learned about loss and how it affects us. Finding my own truth, I was growing and growing. I allowed inspiration, information, and resources to come to me and empower me to develop understanding and empathy. This enabled me to facilitate a holistic process of growth and development not only for the dying, but also the living.

Every patient I witnessed living until the moment of death gave me a deeper understanding of life, death, loss, and grief. My own spiritual journey led me to the Ramtha School of Ancient Wisdom. This training has empowered and allowed me to remember who I really am and to express my own divinity freely. I am so grateful to Ramtha for teaching me about quantum theory and helping me experience it, for assisting me in the understanding of the brain and how to develop it, and most of all, for showing me how to experience unconditional love!

One of the things that always saddens me is when a patient asks, "Where is my spirit? How will I know it?" as if one's spirit is something we only pick up when we die.

Throughout my journey of discovery, I learned that each of us is born as a whole person made up of body, mind, emotion, and spirit. We have to live and grow and heal in those four quadrants.

So many of us grow physically and mentally. We are always learning something new. Some of us even start a spiritual journey of discovery, yet never complete it.

Emotionally, we have all seen immaturity popping its ugly head at the wrong time and wrong place, often boycotting our dreams, forcing us to come face to face with our feelings - often while we are facing the deepest adversaries of our lives.

We do not have to wait until we die before we address all the emotional wounds, unfinished business, and immaturity. Every day we get the opportunity to review our lives and do things better or differently than yesterday.

I have been running self-awareness courses once a month for the past fifteen years. I have never advertised nor have I ever decided who should come and who not. I have developed a deep respect and trust for what I call the "process." The right people are always brought together and are able to share and identify with each other, offering support and encouragement. In quantum science, it is referred to as "frequency specific," meaning we are connected by our frequencies. I have witnessed groups come together who have similarities from characteristics to past events, from habits to careers. No one could plan or organize that! "Process" wants us to grow, heal, shine and reach our fullest potential. Yet because we get hurt in life by people and events, we lose our trust and start withdrawing from this "process." Thus life becomes tough and lonely.

It is my aim to introduce people to this amazing "process" and allow them to see how they can grow, heal and realize they are never alone!

I agree with Ramtha when he tells us that we have forgotten who we really are. We have been brainwashed to believe that we are evil sinners and that "God" is outside of us...confusing and leaving us feeling empty and worthless. Many scriptures, philosophies and religions teach that the body is a temple. If this is true, then surely there must be something "divine" living inside.

We come to a point when we must ask ourselves: "When do we get to know and express that "divine" something?"

Our spirit is always present. From the moment of birth, it silently witnesses our every move... when we enjoy a delicious meal, when we engage in a hot argument, when we close our door for the night. Our spirit is part of it all—it does not sit and wait outside...

Our spirit is where we can start connecting to our passion!

Have you ever observed someone doing mundane tasks...like sweeping the road...yet there is passion present one can see, feel, and experience. Spirit is in action! Getting in touch with that divine presence ignites us and inspires others!

The journey of self-discovery is the richest journey one can encounter and self-awareness is the greatest investment you can make in yourself.

Death, illness, and adversity are worthy teachers!

It is when we are sick that we want to be well. It is when we have the flu that we quickly start taking vitamins. It is when we are dying that we want to live!

Life is the greatest school and adventure. Life is full possibilities to expand, grow, and express ourselves. Every day we can deepen our understanding…our ability to love, allow, and forgive. Every day we are contributing to the Mind of God by embracing our experiences, carrying the wisdom forward and letting the pain go.

Ramtha teaches us the discipline to "create our day," reminding us that we are the creators of our own reality and we alone can change by focusing on what we want to experience and become.

I love who I am becoming!

I love that I am more than my body, my past, and emotions. I love the passion and wisdom my spirit is revealing to me.

May you, too, find that inner connection with your passion.

*Afrikaans word for Grandmother

About the Author

Marisa Wollheim is the honorary director and trainer of Hospice in the West. Her involvement of twenty years has given her a wealth of experience and knowledge. Her wisdom has come from walking a path with dying people and their loved ones, who in turn have inspired and taught her how to live and appreciate life. She is an inspirational, motivational, and confident speaker. Her presence demands the highest respect, yet her humbleness is felt. Marisa is not afraid to confront and own her or her adversaries weaknesses. On her personal journey of growth, she has trained with Dr Elisabeth Kubler-Ross, as a psycho-neuro-immunologist.

She is a student of the Ramtha School of Enlightenment and her passion is facilitating and empowering people, reminding them of their divinity. Widowed two years ago, Marisa has three beautiful adult children: Dominique, Clinton, and Cindy.

Marisa Wollheim may be contacted via:
P O Box 113 Magaliesburg 1791
South Africa
+27 766 49 39 89
Marisa@hospicewest.org.za

It's Never Too Late

APRIL AIMEE ADAMS

Some people know what they want to do with their lives when they're very young. When I was eleven, I wanted to be a movie star. I had it all planned. I would wear fancy clothes and high heels. I would be famous and popular.

When I was twelve, I had my first taste of an alcoholic beverage. It tasted horrible so I spit it out. But it didn't take long for me to realize the up side to drinking alcohol. I had self-esteem issues and was terribly shy, and when I drank, I felt beautiful and confident. I wasn't paralyzed with fear over what others thought of me.

Drinking caused all kinds of problems throughout my school years, including a DUI and a few days in juvenile hall when I was seventeen. I had no boundaries and no direction in life.

Then I started college, and once again I had my life all planned out. I would be an advertising executive or a big shot at one of the local casinos. I would graduate at twenty-one, build my career until I was thirty, then get married and have kids when I was thirty-three. I was more excited than I'd ever been.

College started out well. My grades were higher than the average and I was having a great time. Unfortunately, shortly after I started my sophomore year, drinking became my first priority and I flunked out of college.

I had various jobs during this time including fast food restaurants and telemarketing firms. I also had a habit of getting drunk at company parties, making a fool of myself, and then switching jobs because of it.

When I was nineteen, I was tired of switching jobs. I wanted a career. I decided I wanted to be a flight attendant because I loved flying and it seemed like a job I could handle and enjoy. For months I went to a school which specialized in airline professions, and then I sent resumes to every airline in existence. Once I was flying, my life would be everything I wanted it to be.

Finally, an airline called me for an interview. I drank heavily beforehand, and when I arrived I looked and felt terrible. I couldn't function and I couldn't answer their questions. I didn't get the job and no other airlines called me.

When I was twenty-five, I took a job as a contract administrator for a local homebuilder. I was responsible for overseeing the contracts we had with the subcontractors who actually built the homes, and because I was so analytical, I was great at it. Finally, I had a job I enjoyed and could see myself remaining there for years to come.

Almost a year later, on the fourth of July, I went to the Santa Fe Station Hotel and Casino to play keno and watch the fireworks. I drank too much and blacked out.

I woke up in the hospital, naked with a catheter. The nurse said my blood alcohol level was about .40 and I should've been dead. I told myself I was never going to drink again.

I was angry at myself for risking a job I really loved, and more frustrated than ever at my inability to control my drinking.

A week later, my boss arranged for me to attend a computer training class. Before the class started, I drank a whole bottle of vodka. During the first hour of class, I blacked out. I woke up naked in the hospital with a catheter again. It was *déjà vu*. The nurse told me I'd crashed into a gas pump and totaled my car. She also said my blood alcohol level was about .40 and I should've been dead. Another *déjà vu*.

I told my boss I'd gotten sick in the middle of class and had to leave. I promised myself I would never drink again—and this time I meant it. I was tired of the problems alcohol was causing me. I was going to start anew.

A couple of days later I started drinking again. At this point, I just gave in. I stopped questioning why I couldn't control my drinking. It didn't seem to matter anymore. Nothing did. The bigger my desire to quit, the more difficult it became. I was past the point of even trying. I came to believe alcohol would likely kill me one way or another; I just wanted it to happen quickly. The next few days were a blur. I went through the motions, but inside I felt I was already dead.

Each day before work, I drank a bottle of vodka. Then I went to the grocery store at lunchtime for more vodka. My desire for food diminished.

On August 5, 1994, I was smashed by the time I got to work. The president of the company—my boss's boss—drove me home because I was too drunk to do it myself.

I recall being on the floor with him standing over me. I pulled at his pants leg and said, "Everyone *knows* you're having an affair with your secretary."

"I'm leaving," he said.

I pulled on his pants even harder. "You're not going anywhere," I said. "You're staying right here with me!"

He kicked free of my grip and walked to the living room. I tried to grab a kitchen chair to prop myself up, but it didn't work. After a few unsuccessful attempts, I sank back to the floor. I heard the front door slam shut—then I passed out.

When I came to, I was crying and telling a woman behind a desk I didn't want to lose my job. I was at Monte Vista, a hospital which offers programs to help addicts and alcoholics recover. The woman was trying to convince me to admit myself. I insisted I couldn't because my boss would fire me.

"If you don't admit yourself," the woman said, "you're going to lose a lot more than your job, April. You're going to lose your life. You will die." Finally, I agreed to enter the hospital.

From my first day in rehab, I maintained a positive attitude. It was refreshing to have boundaries and limits. I learned I didn't have to escape life by using addictive substances anymore. I no longer needed to be paralyzed with fear trying to hide the shame of my thoughts, words, actions, or the fact that I exist. I realized I am a beautiful person, worthy of life, love, and happiness. I learned a lot about myself and my alcoholism and I quit drinking for good.

After I got out of the hospital, I became a real estate agent. It was great—at first. I was showing houses and making a ton of money. After a few years, the stress of the business got the better of me and I began thinking about a different career. I knew I wanted to quit the business, but what did I want to do with my life?

Then, I had a friend who used marijuana daily and sought help at Monte Vista, the rehabilitation hospital I'd entered years before. She asked me to attend a group meeting with her on family night.

One of the patients at the meeting was a teenager addicted to Oxy-Contin. His mother sat next to him, beside herself with grief. She was a kind person, but it was painfully obvious her heart was broken. Her son said little, but when he spoke he seemed at wit's end. He'd lied, cheated, and stolen to support his addiction, but he couldn't get his mother to understand that he couldn't help it. He explained that his addiction controlled his mind and body, but she couldn't believe her little boy had turned out so bad. She said she'd lost love for the boy; he seemed like a stranger.

The therapist explained that her little boy was still inside, but he was under lock and key. He said the youth was a slave to his addiction, which controlled his thoughts and actions. As tragic as everything was, she was relieved to understand that it wasn't her son lying, cheating, and stealing—it was the addict inside of him. Her little boy was still there and might be freed by treatment.

As I sat listening to her heartbreak, a light bulb in my head switched on. I looked at the facilitator and thought, "*I could do this. I want to do this.*"

Finally, at the age of thirty-seven, I knew what I wanted to be when I grew up. I decided to become a therapist for young people who were chemically dependent. Even if I couldn't get addicts to stop drinking or using drugs, I could at least educate their families that they weren't bad people, they were just temporarily possessed by the monster called addiction. After all, I knew firsthand what such possession was like. I felt exhilarated. I had a plan to help others; my years of suffering wouldn't have been in vain.

I asked the facilitator of the meeting how to become a counselor and he said the community college had a great two-year degree. When I went to the college, the academic counselor informed me the new rules stated a person had to have a four-year degree to become a counselor. I asked him, "How can I possibly start a four-year degree at the age of thirty-seven?"

He said, "If you never start, you'll never succeed. Start now."

I felt a fresh, powerful energy flowing through me as I thought about the possibilities ahead. I'd never felt so much passion and I couldn't wait to start my journey.

I began by taking core classes at the community college. I put my hair in a ponytail and wore flip flops, trying to fit in with the eighteen-year-olds in my classes. I had to learn a new language because phrases like, "What up, dawg," and "My bad," sounded Greek to me.

I finished the core classes and tried to transfer to UNLV. They still had me under suspension for flunking out two decades earlier, so I began my coursework at a different university.

I was nervous the first day because the other students seemed smarter and more confident than me. Like me, they were older than the typical university student, but I still felt out of place. Even worse, at the end of each five-week course I had to give an oral presentation in front of the whole class.

The more classes I took, the more comfortable I became with making presentations. I learned I was capable of overcoming my fears. I didn't need to avoid people, places, or situations. I needed to meet my fears head on and everything would be okay.

I was earning straight A's and I was on top of the world. Finally I had a purpose in life. Nothing was going to stop me. I didn't have to be pushed by fear anymore. I could decide what I wanted and go after it. I didn't need to passively sit in and watch my life go by. I could write my own play and decide how my story developed. I graduated summa cum laude in 2009 with a degree in psychology at the age of forty-one.

There are a couple of lessons I learned.

1. It's never too late to follow your dreams, or to come up with new ones.
2. Once you find a path that speaks to you, the fortitude and passion follows naturally and easily.

When that happens, nothing can stop you.

About the Author

After struggling with addiction for many years, April Aimee Adams turned her life around. Owner of Rodnee Books, LLC, she has published an autobiography called *That Don't Make Ya Bad: A Memoir of Addiction.*

Besides writing, April spends her time taking care of her ten-year-old twins. Her main goal in life is to help those who struggle with addiction. She wants people to understand that people are not their addictions and the true self is still inside them. They are controlled by the monster of addiction, but they can possibly be freed with treatment, which includes self-discovery and personal growth.

April Aimee Adams may be contacted via:
Rodneebooks.com
P.O. Box 750695, Las Vegas, NV 89136
(702) 530-9610
april@rodneebooks.com

Journey to Wellness on the Cranium-to-Cardio Causeway

JAN MILLS

Life is a journey, complete with detours, points of interest, bumpy roads, and some jet speed travel, as well. I've travelled north to points beyond the Arctic Circle, south to Australia, to Europe and Asia, but the furthest and most important journey I've travelled, and continue to travel, is an inner voyage from my head to my heart. I call it the Cranium to Cardio Causeway.

As a result of being diagnosed with Multiple Sclerosis (MS) in 1986, I'm passionate about my work as a health coach and I'm especially proud of my contribution in 2010 as a medical pioneer with a breakthrough treatment. I have enjoyed a successful, truly heart-based career that has been fulfilling and rewarding. This helped me evolve from the cerebral focus of my life when I was completely estranged from my emotions and body. Life gave me a crash course in altering that route, and always reminds me to consider the needs of the heart.

During my university years, I was headed in the direction of a double-major in Business and Sociology. My impatience with the academic route left me much more interested in the destination than the journey. I researched local companies in advertising and PR. Then I selected one, strutted confidently into the president's office and offered to work for free for two weeks. I was sure the company would want to hire me. I was offered a full-time position and quit attending university the next day. This was an intentional detour on the career highway.

Everything seemed to be going great in this new corporate culture. I was working hard and playing hard, too. I purchased a brand-new car, lived in a gorgeous condo, and thought I had it all. There was one annoyance, my feet kept going completely numb. Denial was a captivating process that got me to the next destination. I hoped my physiotherapist would know the right solutions to allow me to continue the drive along the career highway I was so enjoying. After a few treatments, she suggested I see my physician.

I delayed going to the doctor until the numbness moved up my legs and I started to lose my coordination. The struggle was becoming more significant. Walking between the displays of the 1986 World Expo felt like I had been walking for days through the desert. My career focus, however, reduced the urgency of the physical symptoms.

When I went to see my doctor, she told me to pack my things and go to the hospital. I admitted myself that night because my legs were becoming paralyzed. The numbness moved up my torso like a tight elastic band and I began having difficulty moving my arms. What was going on? Each day brought more tests and more paralysis. As I lay on the table while the medical team did a spinal fluid tap, I realized that my vehicle was shutting me down and forcing a detour on the journey I had planned. The neurologist suspected I had multiple sclerosis (MS). I was riding a roller coaster of emotions…confusion, shock, motivation, and determination.

I knew nothing about MS. The neurologist said it was a mysterious and progressive disease that could involve paralysis and/or blindness which could be either temporary or permanent. He felt the paralysis I was experiencing would probably go away if I would take a heavy dose of a corticosteroid called Prednisone. The medical community was unclear as to what caused MS or how to cure it. The physicians were certain that it almost always involved extreme fatigue.

I wondered if this disease and potential paralysis would permanently park my joy of international travel, would limit the possibility of marrying one day and would direct my life journey into a forced dependence on others for help. The next few weeks in the hospital were focused on regaining my mobility and potential independence. I felt confident I would recover and became motivated by that optimism and a determination to ensure that this detour wouldn't put an end to my career and lifestyle plans.

The constant fatigue redirected my career to the route of entrepreneurism. Two of my largest clients helped me start my own company and gave me their support. A television producer asked if I would like to work on a travel series which he was producing. The project was very challenging and exciting and involved travel to many other countries. Due to this opportunity, I attracted an international airline as a client - I felt I had truly arrived! After a few months, my primary contact at the airline resigned to start his own event marketing company and we merged our companies to become business partners. Several months later, we began dating and soon we married - merging all aspects of our lives together to create projects and a lifestyle on an even larger scale. For years it was very exciting and extremely profitable, yet it was a very intense marriage, like driving along a winding road with some very steep cliffs on the sides. The highly stressful life partnership couldn't survive and ultimately ended in divorce.

My company negotiated sponsorships to build strategic alliances as well as produced international events and television shows worldwide. The clients and events ranged from large corporations to a small Canadian-based circus company that we hired for its first international show (Cirque du Soleil.) Over the next ten years, I continued to experience paralyzing and blinding MS attacks every eight to ten months, yet I always managed to see the silver lining in life; when my legs were numb from the MS, it was an ideal time to get them waxed! Being an invisible disease, the MS could be hidden from most people until an attack was really severe. I would then disappear for a while and give direction by telephone from my bed. I was desperate to prove that being a young businesswoman who had been diagnosed with a degenerative disease was not going to limit me. (That need was both my strongest ally and at times my greatest nemesis.)

I learned about the correlation between my thoughts and my physical health at a holistic retreat center. I was part of an international team that delivered a program entitled "Developing a Holistic Center." I was also their representative on the board and later elected president of Canadian Business for Social Responsibility. It was an honor to work with so many companies that were heart-based in their ethical business practices and soon I was consulting to holistic centers in other countries. This grounded me in a whole new level of conscious and responsible business development, which I included for-profit philanthropy as a new approach to our corporate economy. My business was thriving. I employed people who shared my values, and I felt confident that I was "making a difference."

A few days after Princess Diana's tragic death in 1997, I received a phone call urging me to produce an event. I was encouraged to make it a fundraiser for one of Diana's charities. While driving to the theatre on the night of the gala, I was hit head-on by a drunk driver. I reflect back on the irony of the situation - nearly killed in a head-on collision en route to a tribute for a princess killed in a car accident.

My body seemed visibly undamaged on the outside, but the head injury, whiplash, vertigo, and MS symptoms continued to worsen and soon I was unable to stand or walk on my own. The more I worried about speeding up my recovery, the more it slowed down. When I was finally able to stand, it was two steps forward, one step back. Seven months later, I was a passenger in a car that was hit by another vehicle. As I encountered another severe setback, I wondered what life was trying to teach me.

When I was told by my neurologist that he wasn't sure I would ever regain the use of my right leg, it seemed clear to me that all the pharmaceuticals were not working and I took my health into my own hands. I researched alternative treatments and integrative medicine, instead of relying exclusively on the traditional medical system.

A decade of taking corticosteroids had progressively damaged my bone density. I was diagnosed with advanced osteoporosis in my hips and neck. Again, I reflect on this as the price I paid for taking that particular route on my journey - my vehicle was wearing down.

I found some relief from the pain with acupuncture. I hired a personal trainer as I had become quite concerned about the muscular atrophy from the months of limited mobility. As a result, I began to do research and developed a keen interest in health and wellness.

Good things sometimes result from bad situations. As a fundraiser for the Canadian Cancer Society (CCS) I was honoring my sister who had lost her life to that disease. Martin Mills, the volunteer president of our local chapter of the CCS was also motivated to make a difference in honor of his deceased wife, Debra.

When Martin and I met, it was as close to love at first sight as you can imagine. We soon married. The fact that he had persevered through his first wife's struggle with a terminal illness gave me a significant degree of hope and comfort that he was very different from my first husband and that our love could see us through any challenges that might come our way.

We took a Mediterranean cruise for our honeymoon, the culmination of a life-long dream. Fifteen years earlier when I was diagnosed, I feared international travel might no longer be a possibility in my life - that I'd never see the pyramids of Egypt, or the other great wonders of the world. But there I was at the Acropolis and so I challenged myself to walk up all the steps as a statement of triumph over my perceived limitations. Martin followed behind me, carrying my wheelchair in case I tired, and the entire way up, he hummed the theme from Rocky. When I made it all the way to the top, I did a little victory dance and gazed down proudly at the staggering accomplishment. Martin was part of my victory.

Although I felt that my health recovery hit a plateau, I continued to be free of paralyzing and blinding MS attacks. I was unshakeable in my commitment to attend trainings that were educational and inspirational. When I followed my hearts passion, a health coaching business evolved. I was exhilarated to learn the founder of USANA, Dr. Myron Wentz, was building a holistic medical center for the diagnosis and treatment of degenerative diseases. Finally, the dream came true. I attended a workshop with Dr. Denis Waitley where the participants were given the opportunity to join him on a tour of Dr. Myron Wentz's newly-opened Sanoviv Medical Institute in Rosarito, Mexico.

I remember sitting and weeping in Sanoviv's Education Center after listening to an introductory presentation. My tears were of appreciation and admiration that finally someone had created a holistic center that truly embodied the concept of "holistic." My tears were also a confusion of excitement, curiosity, and sadness as I thought of how this would be a place where I would one day receive something invaluable and truly priceless for my own health. The excitement was mixed with gratitude for having found a licensed hospital with a five-star spa! Yet sadness accompanied the thought I might not be able to afford it. Then I remembered that the workshop focus was on goal-setting and there were no limits to what I could achieve. So I rejoined the group on tour, fell in love with the beauty and perfection of this medical retreat, and became clear and determined that I would return to Sanoviv for a two-week medical program.

Between 2001 and 2009, I returned to Sanoviv eight times, each visit holding its own significance and yet, my most important visit came in the spring of 2010.

In November 2009, an exciting announcement was made in the international media that would change the lives of MS patients worldwide. Dr. Paolo Zamboni, a former vascular surgeon in Italy, was motivated by a labor of love for his wife, who had been diagnosed with MS. His discovery of blockages in the veins of people diagnosed with MS became known throughout the world as Chronic Cerebrospinal Venous Insufficiency (CCSVI) and is nicknamed "The Liberation Treatment."

When I learned the testing and treatment procedures were not available in North America and people were travelling to Europe for them, I was motivated and focused as I had never been before. My husband and I chose to share what we had discovered with the medical team at Sanoviv to whom I had entrusted my health for nearly a decade. Dr. Wentz purchased the specialized diagnostic equipment, sent part of the team to Italy for training, and called to tell me the great news - they were ready for me to come to Sanoviv for CCSVI testing and potential treatment. As I sat in my wheelchair, I was so excited. I had waited 24 years for a glimmer of hope like this. I was about to be the first to receive the tests. I had blockages in my left and right jugular veins of 25% and 85% respectively, and a 100% blockage in my azygos vein. I chose to undergo the risk of venoplasty and was successfully treated for CCSVI.

After the CCSVI procedure, I immediately had more feeling in my feet and hands, which had felt numb for decades. In the recovery room, my husband and physician noticed how significantly my speech had improved. The next day I was able to walk independently and felt the grass between my toes, a sensation I hadn't experienced in decades. I parked my wheelchair, walker, and cane. With excitement I declared that this was "one small step for Jan, one giant leap for mankind." When I returned home, I was thrilled to start driving my car and playing golf again...pleasures I had been unable to do for nearly two years. This sense of independence was liberating for both my husband and me! I wanted to shout to all MS patients everywhere that they could do what I did, but Elaine Pace, president of Sanoviv, reminded me at my two-month follow-up that it was possible not all CCSVI patients would have the same results. She put it well with her acronym YMMV, which meant "Your Mileage May Vary."

My CCSVI experience helped me believe that everything happens for a reason. I was able to further assist the Sanoviv medical team in designing what is said to be the finest CCSVI program in the world.

Perhaps part of the reason for my health challenges was to make that journey and inspire others. Dr. Denis Waitley once said, "Chase your passion, not your pension." My passion for sharing the CCSVI message with Sanoviv and then with others resulted in multiple media interviews for my husband, Martin, and me about the significant changes in our lives as a result of the procedure and the ongoing follow-up program. Since my CCSVI treatment, I have coached more than 1,000 other individuals diagnosed with MS helping them to see there is an exciting ray of hope for an otherwise debilitating disease.

I am as passionate about sharing the message of proactive disease prevention for healthy people as I am for those who have already been diagnosed with a degenerative illness. My heart feels strongly about the value of education for healthy people to maintain good health. I am passionate about nutritional supplements as well as doing thorough research when entrusting your health to a medical team and facility.

I marvel at the fact that the journey from my head to my heart seemed the most difficult for me to navigate...and that is the exact route that the CCSVI blockage took.

Now I know there are no limits on life's journey when you truly pursue your passion and move from your head to your heart along the Cranium to Cardio Causeway!!

About the Author

Jan Mills is an international speaker, author, and health coach. She is featured in *Waking Up the West Coast: Healers and Visionaries* and is a contributing writer to numerous books including the *Heart Book Series: Heart of a Woman, Heart of the Holidays*, and *Heart of a Woman in Business*.

As a professional speaker, Jan has a gift for inspiring her audiences and clients while educating them. Her successful business career and personal triumph over adversity have served an impressive client list that appreciates her wisdom coupled with a witty sense of humor. Her passion for a holistic approach to health and her years of research and training in the wellness industry have demystified and simplified health care choices for people from three continents.

Jan Mills may be contacted via:
jan@janmills.net
www.janmills.net
www.janandmartin.usana.com
www.sanoviv.com - please quote referral code JM100172
Jan Mills & Associates
3948 Gallagher's Parkway
Kelowna, BC Canada V1W 3Z8
(250) 979-0008

Inspiration

A strong passion for any object will ensure success, for the desire of the end will point out the means.

—*William Hazlitt*

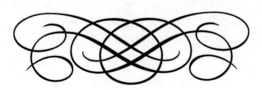

My True American Dream

JUSTINA RUDEZ

I was born the youngest of 8 children in a part of Yugoslavia which is now a country called Montenegro. This is located in South Eastern Europe, bordered by Croatia.

My parents had a small farm and were very poor. My father passed away suddenly when I was only 1 ½ years old leaving my mother alone with no job skills to support all those children. We struggled to get by with what little we could for the next 10 years. Money was so critical when I was smaller that while I did attend school back in Croatia, I never even had a pencil or paper. The blessing from that was I learned to memorize extremely well!

Finally one of my brothers, Tony, who was 18 at the time, went on a search to find a better life for us all. My mother was heartbroken that he was gone. It was extremely difficult for her. The farm was the only life she had known but she knew he was right and she wanted something better for her children. Eventually, Tony convinced my mother to immigrate to Italy, taking all but the two oldest children. They were grown and chose to stay behind in the only home they had ever known.

Once we arrived in Italy, the 6 children along with my mother all lived in one room in a boarding house for another 9 months. Then we moved on to New York, settling in the Bronx where we all got various jobs in factories and sweat shops.

In the 'old country', it was customary for girls to be put into arranged marriages by the age of 15. My mother, being from the 'old country' decided I would not be going to school in America. I was never allowed to go back to school. At 13, I told the factory owner that I was

17 in order to get a job. I was working full time sewing coats for only $38.00 a week!

The Italian women I worked with in the factory took me under their wings and wanted to take care of me. They were always saying to me, "Justina, you are killing yourself. You need to go to school." My dream was to be a hairdresser. Even before I met these women, I would stand outside of hair salons and gaze through the window fantasizing about how great it would be to be able to do hair!

The Italian women introduced me to two girls that owned a hair salon and after talking with them, I made the decision to be a hair dresser. I was so very excited. Bit by bit, I purchased everything I needed to start to the school. There was one MAJOR drawback; I was too young to enroll without my mother's permission! When I first asked her, she was adamantly against it! In fact, it took over 4 months of begging and pleading with her to change her mind! I asked everyone who had any influence with her to help me convince her. It was only after one of my brothers said he would make sure I didn't get into any trouble or tarnish the family name that she finally relented and allowed me to go!

That first hurdle was difficult; the second hurdle was even tougher! COST...

In our family, we all turned our entire earnings every week over to the 'family pool.' My brother was in charge of all the finances for the family and when I asked him for the $1000.00 needed for the tuition, he told me there wasn't any money for hairdressing school. Because of this, I had to keep my full time job and attend school at night and weekends. What normally could have been done in 7 months took me 2 years of dedication and hard work to accomplish! I was determined to finish!

I spoke three languages fluently; however, my English was not so good. Since I had not been allowed to go to school, I had difficulty reading and understanding the text in English.

At the time of finals for graduation, I was scared about not being able to read and understand the questions on the final exam! I couldn't take a chance on missing any questions and I didn't know exactly what questions might be on the test...so I did the next best thing... I memorized the WHOLE BOOK! My classmates knew I had a hard time reading English, so imagine their shock when I was the first one to finish the test! They were even more shocked when it was announced that I had passed!

I married at 18, opened my first salon at 21. Within a few short years, I had 3 beautiful children, and was living what I thought was the 'American Dream.' The truth of the matter was that all I did was work. I had no time for my family, much less for myself!

I didn't want to raise my children in the streets of New York City so in 1985, my husband and I decided to move to Florida. I sold my salon in New York and we moved. I still needed to work, so I joined a network marketing company thinking this would give me more time to spend with my children and the freedom to be the mom I had always wanted to be. I soon found out the hard way that not all network marketing companies are created equal! I needed to make money. Once again, I opened a hair salon. In order to be a successful business owner, I was soon back to working 60 hours a week and not spending any time with my children.

As a hairdresser, I became interested in looking for ways to maintain optimal health. One day, a true blessing came knocking at my door, although I didn't consider it a blessing at the time. Carol, one of my stylists in the salon introduced me to USANA nutritional supplements. USANA was the answer I was looking for, in more ways than one!

Like many people, I was too busy at first to ever recognize what an opportunity USANA was! It was a network marketing group and I wasn't interested. Carol asked me to attend a meeting and I was too busy. Then she asked if she could sell USANA in the salon since she was not an employee but rented booth space. I told her it was fine as long as she didn't pester the rest of us to join! (We've all heard that before, haven't we?) So she just went about her business. Carol was a good friend whom I had known a long time and I started feeling bad about how negatively I had reacted. As time went by, I decided that I would be more pleasant about it so I expressed an interest in learning more about USANA.

Coincidently, her sponsor was sitting in her chair at that very moment! We agreed to meet for lunch, which I was dreading and feeling like I was stuck. I told them I wasn't interested in doing the whole business but they could sign me up for whatever would help Carol. I really had no plans to do any of this for me; I thought I was just helping Carol out! Funny how things can change!

I didn't even decide what the first shipment would be. I left that up to Carol! Soon a large package was delivered and I thought "What the heck am I going to do with all this stuff? Well...I might as well go ahead and try it since it is already here."

It didn't take long; I started noticing that I was feeling better than I had in years! I had taken many different vitamins over the years and never experienced anything like this before. I wasn't sure whether I should attribute these changes to the new vitamins or something else? But what?

Since I had a 'captive' audience each and every day in my chair at the salon, I started wondering out loud to them. I was having conversations about how wonderful these new products were making me feel and the 'word of mouth' spread! Soon checks were coming in the mail and I still didn't know how it all worked! My interest was definitely peaked and I decided to dedicate myself to a company that not only had terrific products but was helping people. I was thrilled with their terrific compensation plan. Remember, I'd already had a previous experience that didn't turn out so good!

After the first year, I was making a good income from the sale of the products. I LOVED the products and talked to everyone I met about how wonderful USANA was. For someone who had never even been allowed to attend school, this gave me the opportunity of a lifetime! By the third year, I was very successful with my USANA business. I happily 'retired' from my salon to FINALLY have a life of my own!

Hair was something I had always wanted to do and I had been very passionate about. The decision to quit doing hair came from several different things. Over the years, it had been hard on my body and affected my health. The pain of carpel tunnel from years of using my hands, the cough from the chemicals in the salon and the long hours of not being able to spend any time with my family all contributed to the decision to 'retire' and embrace USANA as my full time occupation.

I shifted the passion I had for hair to a new and even more exciting passion of helping people live healthier lives and helping people achieve what I had. I realized that what I had found was the TRUE American dream! This was the perfect business. It didn't just pay me for my time. As long as I worked hard, it paid me over and over again! My passion was helping others and I found a way to do that with USANA. By helping others, my life has changed as well.

Was I an overnight success? No. Just like getting through hair school and building my salon business was not an overnight success, this took time and work as well. I worked hard, believed in and loved the product 100%. I shared my story with everyone I met. I didn't give up. I stayed focused on my goals and put in the necessary time to build a solid foundation. I focused on obtaining my MBA (massive bank account), much like many others who went to college to earn their degrees. I still continue this same formula and continue to live my dreams as I grow!

I wouldn't be the person I am today without USANA. This company and its products have not only changed my life, but the lives of my family members as well. I was able to teach my children about a better life, too. My oldest daughter is now a Ruby level director with the USANA company and well on her way to enjoying the same lifetime of health and wealth as myself.

The added benefits with USANA of amazing trips, cruises and travel have given me many priceless memories that I will always cherish.

Most importantly, I have the opportunity to donate every year to the Children's Hunger Fund which is very near and dear to my heart. I will never forget what it is to be poor and sometimes hungry as well. Of all the awards that I have received, the Children's Fund award is the closest to my heart. I didn't do this alone. I did it with the dedication and support of an amazing team.

Hard work pays off! With USANA, hard work pays off over and over and over again, instead of just one time. I never have to trade time for money again while killing myself trying to do it! And I have all the paper and pencils I can ever use!!!

ABOUT THE AUTHOR

Justina's story today is very different from where it began, when she was a child growing up in Croatia. After Justina's father passed away when she was just over a year old, her mother struggled to care for Justina along with her seven siblings.

At the age of 12, Justina and five of her siblings convinced their mother to immigrate to Italy. Then it was on to New York, where she began working in a sweatshop to help support her family. After several years, Justina opened her first hair salon. Eventually, Justina left her hairdressing business and shifted her focus to network marketing. She is a member of USANA's elite Million Dollar Club. Justina has a passion for mentoring others and helping them achieve success.

Justina Rudez may be contacted via:
www.Usanaforyou.tv
www.Justina.justinarudez.com
Justina@justinarudez.com
(407) 497-4757

Leap of Faith

ANN PARENTI

In *Measure for Measure*, Shakespeare once wrote, "Our doubts are traitors that make us lose the good we oft might win, by fearing to attempt."

For many years now, I have subscribed to that quote and I believe I am beginning to actually embrace it on a deeper level.

Over the last few years, I have been on a journey of self-realization. I didn't mean to take this journey; in fact, I would call myself the accidental tourist. However, I have become driven and some would say passionate about this trip. The odd thing about this autumn holiday...I seem to require very little baggage.

Passion—an interesting word, as words go. What the word brings to my mind currently is an actual shift in perception. As I release my hidden passions or creative nature which I have kept buried inside myself for many years, I feel like a floodgate has opened. I am not sure if I will be able to contain the flood waters once the river is allowed to flow its own natural course. I must have faith that all will flow smoothly and I will not stand as a barrier in my own sea of creativity. I must also strive for balance in my personal and professional lives and practice lifeboat skills with those loved ones who are in my daily life.

Through a series of events which occurred over the last couple of years, I have slowly released my creative self from the shadows of doubt. When the economic world around us appeared to be dramatically changing, I realized it was an opportunity...a gift to pursue my hidden passions.

136

Actually, it began about four years ago with the idea of creating a CD.

As Promised sprang from that conception. The music was inspired by *A Course in Miracles*. Currently, I perform at charity events, churches, and organizations to help others experience healing with my music. Then, I was inspired to create a seminar series called *POSSIBILITIES*. I felt a desire to help people during these challenging times, to overcome their limited beliefs about themselves and the world as they perceive it. Now the writer in me has been unleashed. I was invited to author a chapter in the book *Life Choices: Putting the Pieces Together*. It was a very wonderful and rewarding experience.

In addition to the new, ever expanding side of me, I still love my original career that I have had for considerable years, Parenti & Associates. This business allows me to surround myself with talented professionals like interior designers, architects, purchasing agents, and hotel owners. The business of offering these highly creative professionals my products and services has always been rewarding and still is to this very day.

However, I felt I was hiding a side of myself. The ego or fear factor overwhelmed the essence and spirit of who I truly am. That was a paralyzing situation until now. I continue to work through the fear and do so daily. I am choosing to release this crippling behavior and forge ahead regardless. I am excited to be on the journey we call life because I have come to realize just how quickly life can elude us. If someone had told me I would be an aspiring singer/songwriter, speaker, and author at this time in my life, I would have said he was off his rocker. I couldn't have scripted this scenario if I tried. The first career I chose took a considerable amount of time to establish and run to the level of service I wanted my firm to offer my clients. If the downturn in the economy had not occurred, I seriously doubt I would have had this time and opportunity to focus on my other gifts. I'm not going to try and whitewash this time in my life. It has been stocked full of uncertainty and sadness, of letting go of what I thought was going to be my career until retirement. I was one of the lucky ones. My firm was grounded and withheld the storm of many causalities as I stood back and watched the fallout occur—the loss of 65 percent of my client base, a result of the lay-offs of many dear friends and clients. My own husband was one of the participants in this recession, and he is still without work. He has been unemployed for over a year now, forced to take an early retirement from the union of which he was a part for over forty years. Still too young to collect social security, this puts a creative slant on how we will create additional income to replace the loss of his salary. He is finding his own creative path as his life continues to adjust to this new situation we all face. The true blessing in all of this is that we have become stronger individuals, more loving and compassionate to each other and those around us who are experiencing similar trials. This fallout has left unscathed very few people with whom we are in contact.

If I can inspire others to change their minds and release the illusionary fear that appears so real at times, to pursue their own passion, then my mission is accomplished. Margaret Shepherd said it best: "Sometimes your only available transportation is a leap of faith."

About the Author

Since 1977, Ann Parenti has lived in Las Vegas and has seen this city grow into the community it is today. Ann owns Parenti & Associates, a manufacturers' representative firm that sells products such as wall covering, fabric, furniture, artwork, and digital artwork to the architectural and design community. She has owned the company since 1987 and enjoys her career. Ann is also a singer/ songwriter and has a CD on the market entitled *As Promised*, music based on *A Course in Miracles*. In 2009, when the economy took a detour, an idea came to her to create a seminar to help her clients and friends who were being displaced and let go. *POSSIBILITIES: The Seminar* was born. Now going into its third year, there is no end in sight. Ann is also featured as one of the authors in the book *Life Choices: Putting the Pieces Together*. Ann has been involved in several association network groups that are related to her career such as NEWH - The Hospitality Industry Network, International Interior Design Association, American Society of Interior Designers, and the Rep Network Group. She recently expanded her networking to groups including Women Networking Together in Las Vegas, WE of Las Vegas, and Kiwanis of Las Vegas Neon Lights. Over the years, Ann has adopted and raised money for many community service projects and recently she has been involved with one most near and dear to her heart, Oasis Center. Ann is happily married to Curtis McCoy and has three stepdaughters and seven beautiful grandchildren.

Ann Parenti may be contacted via:
www.parentiandassociates.com
www.possibilitiestheseminar.com
www.forgottensongproductions.com

The Chapter That Shouldn't Have Been Written

BEA GOODWIN

On June 2nd, 2008, I experienced a loss so piercingly painful that my life's course changed in an instant. My passion, my life's purpose to illuminate and humanize the *disease* of pathological gambling, was so clearly laid out before me, it's as if God himself wrote the script and handed it to me saying, "Bea, This is your work. This is the *why* of your existence."

A few days earlier. I had been sitting vigil in the Intensive Care Unit of the Pinnacle Hospital in Harrisburg, Pennsylvania, my beautiful sister Lanie in a coma, the result of an overdose of Paxil. Every fiber of my being, my very soul, wanted to climb into bed next to my big sister, hold her in my arms, and beg her to come back to me.

My Lanie died four days later. She was fifty-two-years-old. She had beaten lung cancer. Who survives *cancer* only to die ten years later as a result of a disease that defies understanding? Surely God had a glorious plan when he spared her life from cancer. How could she now be dead from a disease that you can't see, has no physiological symptoms, and no obvious signs of illness? It doesn't show up as a lump, a limp, a cough, or a pain. A doctor cannot physically diagnose pathological gambling. The deadly disease is an insidious, inside job.

I am living proof of what anyone who suffers from this malady and comes out the other side of it can tell you. Although you may not be able to physically see or diagnose the disease, the sweeping devastation of pathological gambling is undeniably real.

Whether the root cause was one of nature or nurture, Lanie and I both suffered from the disease of compulsive gambling. Although I was the younger sister I was the first to fall victim to the disease. Throughout the course of my journey of recovery, Lanie was my champion, my cheerleader, my dearest friend, and most trusted confidante.

Lanie did not judge me when I shared my secret with her. She responded as she always did—with loving acceptance. She supported me every step of the way as I struggled with the financial, emotional, and spiritual fallout of my disease. I surrendered completely to the twelve-step recovery program of Gamblers Anonymous and began to rebuild my life.

In September of 2001, my sister called me. Through sobs, she admitted that she, too, was a compulsive gambler: she had gambled away all of her inheritance, was in financial ruin, was filled with shame and self-loathing, and was so afraid!

As a recovering compulsive gambler, I knew that by her admission, Lanie had just opened a pathway that would lead her to a beautiful life blessed beyond measure. We began walking the journey hand-in-hand. I sponsored Lanie until she became acquainted with the Program in her hometown and got grounded in a home group.

After some time in recovery, Lanie left Harrisburg and moved to Las Vegas. The years that Lanie lived near me in Nevada were some of the happiest in my life. Both our parents had passed at young ages, and we sisters clung to each other. We were happy and grateful to be together.

On her second Gamblers' Anonymous "birthday," Lanie gave me a figurine of a joyful woman dancing with abandon. On the back she wrote, *My soul was born in 1955. My spirit found life in 2001! Thank you for your loving guidance and encouragement as I continue to learn the dance of joy! Love, Lanie 9-21-03.* I look at this precious gift daily, and as I gaze upon the dancing diva, I think of what was and what could have been.

Lanie went to great lengths to protect her abstinence. She moved in with Aunt Bea back in Pennsylvania to "better assist" our aunt. I believe it was truly a guise to protect herself from too much idle time and the risk of acting out her addiction. Further, she had self-excluded (voluntarily signed documents precluding her from gambling) in Pennsylvania, New Jersey, and Delaware.

Lanie was building her safety net from a disease she knew could consume her soul. Her decision to move back appeared to be a good one. Living with Aunt Bea was great! She adored her new grandson and remained cancer free. We spoke every week, usually several times. Seemingly, life was good.

The last time I spoke with my sister was Saturday, May 24th, 2008. She started the conversation casually, but there was something in her voice. I insisted we talk for a while.

An emotional and sometimes depressed person, Lanie went on and on about a family matter that was troubling her. I clearly remember her repeating over and over again, "It just breaks my heart."

I responded, "Sis, we all have our own journey in this life and our own lessons to learn. No one has the power to make us feel anything. We choose our feelings and responses. Likewise—others' choices, experiences and lessons are theirs to own and learn from."

What concerned me most was the intensity of her sorrow and the helplessness I heard in her voice. I encouraged her to journal, pray, and be sure to go to a meeting. I invited her to call me again and told her how much I loved her.

I never heard her voice again.

The call I received on Tuesday, May 27, 2008, changed my life forever. It was Aunt Bea saying Lanie seemed to be having a stroke. They were at the hospital and it didn't look good. I immediately began making plans to catch a red-eye flight to Pennsylvania. Within the hour, Aunt Bea called again. The doctors had told her Lanie was suffering from a drug interaction. They had induced a coma to keep her calm, but ultimately she would be fine.

Regardless of whether or not she would be "fine," I could barely focus as I wrapped up a business presentation and flew cross-country late on Thursday night, May 29th. I spoke briefly with the nurses in ICU, and spent the rest of the night keeping vigil at my sister's side. The overall consensus from the nurses on duty was that Lanie would fully recuperate. The induced coma was simply a precaution. So I sat quietly, holding my sister's hand and listening to the beeps and hums, and the drip, drip, drip rhythm moving throughout the ICU.

The next morning a physician explained Lanie's condition to me. She had Serotonin Syndrome from an excess of anti-depressants. Too much of her prescription Paxil, or an innocuous drug interaction with something as simple as the herbal anti-depressant St. John's Wort, taken in addition to her prescription, could have caused the syndrome. Her coma had been induced to circumvent complications like kidney failure or a stroke. Once the serotonin wore off, she would simply wake up.

On day two, a group of physicians began an onslaught of probing and persistent questions. They again mentioned St. John's Wort. "Any chance she was taking this along with the Paxil?" "Has your sister been especially upset lately?" "How's her family life?" "How about work?"

Internal alarms started to sound. I wondered why they were asking so many questions.

"It sounds as if you think this may have been intentional," I said.

The chief physician replied, "I don't know how anyone could possibly have this much serotonin in her body without it being intentional."

This was unfathomable! Yes, Lanie was prone to depression. Yes, she reacted with high emotion at times, but a self-inflicted overdose? No way. Surely, it was simply a miscalculation. I clung to the doctors' statement that she would "wake up when the serotonin wears off."

Only...the serotonin did not "wear off." My Aunt Bea came to me with a sorrowful look of hurt and pain: she'd found a plastic grocery bag overflowing with papers in Lanie's car—ATM receipts from a casino in West Virginia dated May 24th and 25th, 2008.

I can't recall either of us saying a word for some time. We both knew the implications. I was numb, sad, fearful, and angry. Never for one moment did I feel anger toward Lanie. I was angry at a disease that is so cunning, baffling, and powerful that the compulsion to gamble can override all reason, causing only devastation in its wake.

After quietly sitting with my feelings for a time, I whispered in Lanie's ear.

"Sis, I know you've been gambling again. It's going to be okay, honey. The doctors think you may have done this on purpose, but I don't. I think you just didn't want to feel the pain anymore. You're going to be okay, Lanie. You're going to wake up and when you do, we'll get you into treatment. There's nothing to be ashamed of, baby. You don't *ever* have to feel shame or fear with me. There is nothing you could ever do that would make me love you less."

With that, one single tear slid down her cheek. I'll never forget that moment. She heard me. She understood. It was going to be okay. I understood this illness. I had lived it. We had lived it together. We would get through this together, too.

Late that night, an intern came in to attend to my sister. As requested, I handed him a bag containing all of Lanie's medications. After thoroughly examining the contents, he determined none of the pills could have interacted to cause the serotonin syndrome. I then shared the new information I had learned that afternoon.

"I now know more than I did this morning," I said. "My sister is a compulsive gambler, and so am I. I am in recovery and thought she was, too, but I just found out she's been gambling again."

To me, this explained everything—encompassing pain and shame so great my sister had tried to numb herself with anti-depressants. This doctor's response, however, the tone and body language—all of it—is etched in my memory forever. With an inappropriately gleeful tone, and a smile on his face, he looked up at me and asked, "Did she win?"

Did...she...win? Lanie lay in a coma not three feet away from us and he asked if she had *won*?

I was stunned into incredulous silence. The next morning, I was waiting for the gaggle of doctors coming through on grand rounds.

"First of all, the intern who was on duty last night needs to work on his bedside manner," I began. "And I am telling you what I told him. My sister is a compulsive gambler. I thought she was in recovery, but I found out that she's been gambling again in West Virginia."

The group of physicians reacted almost simultaneously, but their responses baffled me.

"Why would she gamble in West Virginia?" "Yeah...that doesn't make any sense; there's gambling right here at Penn National."

On and on they went. Not one word about the fact that Lanie suffered from the disease of compulsive gambling! I was angry and horrified. Who cares *where* she gambled? Clearly, they were oblivious that the key to the mystery of my sister's condition had been revealed!

In the following days, Lanie did not wake up as expected. The doctors became increasingly concerned about her failure to respond. No additional sedation had been administered since the initial dose, so the serotonin should have been flushed from her system. Something was off. Finally, they medically countermanded the induced coma. Lanie's body briefly twitched and moved. Her eyes opened and...nothing. She was unresponsive to verbal commands. She was not visually "tracking."

She was simply not there.

After still more testing, the results were heartbreaking. Lanie had suffered a major brain-stem stroke, which would leave her in a vegetative condition for the rest of her life. Based on this new information, the medical team began frantically ordering a tracheotomy and a feeding tube, as well as a social services consultation for our family to determine nursing home accommodations.

After days of quiet hope and reassurance that Lanie would simply wake up, her hospital room was now a rush of action: physicians urgently relaying orders and nurses rushing about. Every cell in my body was screaming S T O P!

I needed a minute to adjust. Why were they rushing? Lanie was not going anywhere. I just needed time to assimilate this information. My mind was crying out, *Please. Oh, please. Won't you all just leave the room and give me some quiet? I need to be with my sister!*

There was no silence. Everything kept moving until I finally spoke up.

"Everyone just *stop*," I said firmly and loudly. "No one is authorized to do anything until I say so. Got it?"

Silence. They got it. Eventually my mind and heart caught up with the aftershock and I began talking to Lanie again. Whispering in her ear...wondering if the cognitive thought that caused the single tear to roll down her cheek earlier was still present. Was there even a shadow of my sister in there? Still I whispered words of love, knowing her spirit was surely hovering somewhere nearby.

The doctors left us alone, and eventually, I wandered out to the nursing station. The nurses were so nurturing; they were absolute angels. They sat with me, held me, answered my questions honestly, and gave me straightforward feedback. I shared my gut feelings.

I couldn't let my sister "live" like this. Lanie and I both shared the philosophy that our bodies are simply "the car that drives our soul around earth," and she wouldn't want to be stuck in a car that did not run. I spoke with Lanie's grown children. Lanie had a Living Will, and thus we knew her wishes. Through sobs and tear-stung eyes, we all agreed that Lanie would most definitely not want to live like this.

The nurses charted the family's decision.

Throughout those days I was like a lioness protecting her cub, just as I know Lanie would have been for me. The fighting was over and it was time to say goodbye to my best friend. We arranged a time for all of the family and friends and her pastor to gather for a "love circle."

The nurses expected Lanie's passing to be quick, but she hung in for several hours. Throughout, we all stayed with her. A calm came over me, as the Holy Spirit surely must have taken over to guide my actions. I whispered words of love and encouraged my Lanie to 'just let go.'

Curiously, escorting my sister from this life to the next remains the single most humbling and beautiful human experience I've ever had. All focus was on her and my heart was awash with pure love.

When, finally, Lanie's body released, an earsplitting, primal wail filled the space of the hospital room. It was so loud and heartbreaking that for a moment I didn't know where it had come from.

It had come from me. A piece of my heart broke off in that moment as my sister's spirit was fully released.

Now she is at peace.

I vowed then and there that someday I would address the American Medical Association to shine light on the disease of compulsive gambling. They need to know that gamblers have the highest suicide rate of any other addiction. I want them to understand.

Gambling is now legal in forty-eight states in the U.S. Most people do not understand compulsive gambling. Logic says, "Just STOP!" However, pathological gambling, like any addiction, defies logic. It is an illness that is undetectable, silent, and deadly.

Today, I no longer maintain my anonymity. I have a mission to complete. I owe it to Lanie's memory to speak out. I owe it to the physicians and health care professionals to speak out. I owe it to the compulsive gambler who still suffers. And I owe it to the families of compulsive gamblers. It is my calling to be of service and to educate others about this disease: how to spot it—how to help—and where to find help.

Recovering pathological gamblers know that "our disease wants us dead."

If, by speaking publicly about our disease, I can save one "Lanie," mine will have been a life well-lived. No one else will have to write "the chapter that shouldn't have been written."

About the Author

Bea Goodwin has been passionately committed to "helping the compulsive gambler who still suffers," since her own recovery journey began over fifteen years ago. She now dedicates herself fully to her mission of illuminating and humanizing the disease of pathological gambling; bridging the vast gap between the legal, medical, and private sectors and the pathological gambler who still suffers.

She is the founder of Twelve Dollars, (so named to reflect the "abundant mindset" Bea experienced after balancing her checkbook a year into her own recovery journey and joyfully exclaiming that God had "provided for all of her needs PLUS twelve dollars") and spearheads the community advocacy mission "Lanie's Hope," dedicated to enhancing awareness and attracting support for programs serving the needs of the pathological gamblers and their families. Treatment programs and vital resources are available but public funds are severely limited and existing programs have been devastated by repeated budget cuts. Lanie's Hope is dedicated to supporting these services through the non-profit Nevada Council on Problem Gambling and treatment centers throughout the United States.

Bea has been a featured presenter at local and national Gamblers Anonymous conferences as well as the 2011 NV State Association of Family Practitioners and the Nevada State Conference on Problem Gambling. She is following her commitment to reach out to the medical community to enhance understanding of the disease of compulsive gambling, addressing physicians, residents, and medical students alike. She has been featured on Steppin' out Radio and her personal recovery story "Twelve Dollars" was published in the book *Life Choices: Putting the Pieces Together* (Turning Point International, copyright 2010).

Bea Goodwin may be contacted via:
bea@lanieshope.org
www.lanieshope.org
(702) 812-1922

Optimism

*Passion is energy. Feel the power that comes
from focusing on what excites you.*

—Oprah Winfrey

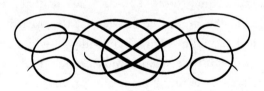

The Soda Fountain

DOTTIE WALTERS

I went to solicit ads for my shopper's column from four merchants in Baldwin Park. I had previously tried to sell an ad to the man who owned the local Rexall Drug store. Every time I'd go in, he was out. He was always out. I could never catch him in.

The four different businessmen told me, "You don't have the man whom we most admire in town in your column. He is the local pharmacist, a fine man and if he's not using your column, then we don't want to be in it either."

I thought, *Oh, my gosh; I must try again! He must be working sometime. If he could just look at it and give me a comment, then I could give it to these merchants who know him and think so much of him.*

The Walters tenacity kicked in. My Scottish blood, inherited from that undaunted grandfather of mine, was moving me toward success. I went back one more time to see if I could talk to that pharmacist. This time as I walked in the front, I could see that the back of the pharmacy was lit up. There I saw him—white hair with the white jacket that they wear. I had my kids with me again. I walked up and said 'Mr. Ahlman, I don't want to sell you anything, I just want you to give me your thoughts on this column. Would you just be so kind as to look at it? The other merchants in town want your opinion. Please, would you?' He shook his head from left to right. His mouth was an upside down U, saying no.

I didn't know if I could make it home pushing the kids in the baby carriage all the way up that hill. I got as far as the soda fountain. There were three empty stools. I sat down on the one closest to me and pulled the kids up close so they wouldn't be in the way. I sat there thinking, *What am I going to do?* The soda jerk came over. I asked him, "How much for your smallest Coke?" It was ten cents. That was all I had, so I laid that out and gave the kids each a straw so they got a little sip. They were thirsty too, breathing all that dust. I must have looked as discouraged as I felt.

Soon two ladies came in and sat down on the stools next to me. The one sitting closest to me turned and said, "What in the world is wrong with you, girl?"

I said, "We are going to lose our home. I've done everything I can think of to do. Everyone thinks so much of Mr. Ahlman, but he won't even give me his opinion on my column. Four merchants turned me away today. Those four would have finished the house payment. I don't want to lose our little house."

The lady said, "You wait right here." First she snatched away the column that I had in my hand. She read every word of it. Then she yelled, "Rueben, get out here!" It was her husband!

Mr. Ahlman, the pharmacist, proved to be truly generous to every charity. So much so, that his wife had taken over that part of the business. I had been talking to the wrong person! I didn't know enough to know to ask who was in charge of that part of the business.

Mrs. Ahlman told her husband, "You give this girl copy for this week. I'll go back and make a check out for two months of ads." I was stunned. Next, Mrs. Ahlman asked me for the names of the four merchants who turned me away. As soon as I gave her their names, she left to place phones calls to each one of them. She returned to tell me that the merchants were waiting to see me. I didn't give up. I looked for the opportunity. This one changed my life.

The biggest opportunities seem to have a special knack of only showing themselves when things seem at their bleakest, when life seems dark and out of options. This is where opportunity becomes visible if you are open to it. At that moment you can ask for the opportunity to present itself. It will be happy to do so. Great opportunities are just waiting for moments like that. Mine was no different.

Einstein was right. Solutions are located at hand. They are very close to you. But you have to go after them. They are not going to sit there by themselves and do it. You've got to do it. Reach out and don't be afraid to go after your dream, because it's waiting for you.

About the Author

While pushing 2 babies in a broken down baby stroller in a rural community with no sidewalks, Dottie Walters began a tiny advertising business. She built that business into 4 offices, 285 employees and 4,000 continuous contract advertising accounts. Dottie sold this large business to concentrate on her own speaking, writing, and the administration of Walters International Speaker Bureau. Since 1978 her own *"Sharing Ideas"* news magazine, was known as the top international publication in the paid speaking-meetings-speakers bureaus world.

A favorite with audiences in the U.S., England, Malaysia, Australia, Japan, Canada, South Africa and Singapore, Dottie spoke on sales, motivation and the world of professional speaking. She was the founder of a professional association for speakers bureaus, known as The International Group of Agencies & Bureaus (IGAB); a founding member of the National Speakers Association, co-founder of NSA Los Angeles Chapter and recipient of IGAB's John Palmer Award for outstanding contributions to the bureau industry.

For information contact:
Michael MacFarlane
Walters Speakers Services
PO Box 398
Glendora, CA 91740
(626) 335-8069

Finding My True North

CHERYL SMITH

Every once in a while, there comes a time in life when you get an empty feeling that won't go away without addressing it. It's the itch to do something different or try something out of the ordinary. It's the desire to be adventurous. It's that nagging, unfulfilled sensation that keeps you up at night wondering, *What if?*

We all have passions in our lives and we deserve to pursue them. We often put practical obligations in our way and use them as excuses for not pursuing our desires, reaching our goals, or achieving our dreams. *I can't do XYZ because I have to work to pay my mortgage, put the kids through school, and support my family.* Okay, I get it. I have similar obligations. I have bills to pay and a family to support, too. Trying to juggle obligation and pursuit of passion can be complicated, but possible if you're open to opportunity.

Maybe you're bored in your job and you need a career change. Maybe it's a relationship you want to get out of. You feel trapped. Maybe you're stressed trying to balance work and family. Maybe you've been thinking about taking dance or music lessons, but you're too embarrassed. You feel an ache, a pain of emptiness underneath the surface that's screaming for attention. You realize the ability to make a living is so routine and easier to do than taking on the challenge and risk of pursuing that which you would love to do, even when you know it's in your best interest. That's the point I was at six years ago—balancing between what appeared normal and a burning desire inside to change my life to be less stressful. It was the perfect time to check my internal compass, reconsider the direction I was heading in my life, make adjustments, and take action. For me, pursuing my passion began with finding my true north.

For nearly ten years, I was a working mother with a daily routine so hectic I can't remember anything meaningful about any given day. I went to work, took my children to and from school, prepared dinner for my family, took the kids to sporting events and music lessons, and then wound down by doing what every working mother does late at night in her free time—clean the house, do laundry, and hopefully, go to bed by midnight. Combine this with the pressures of a hospital marketing job requiring me to be on-call 24/7 and my work never ended. I was tired, stressed, and crabby.

I am of the generation of women who grew up being told by society and pop culture that we must "do it all"—have a family and a career. I believed balance was possible. I grew up learning how to be everything to everyone all of the time. I spent the better part of my adult life trying to achieve this goal. Why? Because that's what I was told I needed to do and I didn't know any better.

At the time of this writing, I am in my forties and life has afforded me enough experiences and wisdom to ask why anyone would want to do it all? Especially, all at the same time? I asked myself how I got where I am. Have I accomplished everything that I've set out to do in my life? What have I done to make a difference? To whom? As I answered these questions, I realized I didn't like the answers.

I described the feeling to my husband one night after our children went to bed. I told him I felt like a pilot off course, blinded by clouds all around me, not knowing which way was up or down and feeling hopelessly lost, but constantly moving. Somewhere in the twenty years between going to college, having a family, building a career, and being a full-time working mother, I lost a sense of me. I lost the pursuit of personal passion in my life. Don't misunderstand, by most accounts I am blessed beyond my worth and don't think I don't know it. I have a wonderful husband and the two most handsome sons on the planet! We have a beautiful home, good health, and enjoy happiness together that others might envy. However, the missing piece for me was personal passion. I had no hobbies, no time for gym workouts or Jazzercise classes, too busy for art, ballroom dance, or crafting courses, no time to learn to speak Italian, no garden, not even a bowling league! I needed a change of direction.

We all have internal compasses guiding our decisions, steering our direction, funneling our thoughts into focused actions, and providing the moral ground on which we stand. We experience life based upon the direction our compass is pointing. How many of us are in control of our internal compass? How many of us have a life plan? Certainly not me. I never put one thought into the overall direction my life was heading or even where I wanted it to go. I felt out of balance, spending too much of my time with work and the stress of managing meaningless activities and not enough time with my family doing the things that brought enjoyment, peace, and fun into my life.

In business marketing, we commonly say, "failure to plan is planning to fail." No wonder I felt unfulfilled. I had no life plan! Who does? Was I really any different than anyone else? I decided to change that.

I began a search for passion. Since I didn't feel I had it in my life, I needed to find out what it looked like. What would I need to do? Where would I find it? When I looked around me, I saw a neighbor who gets up early and rides his marathon racing bicycle every day. That looked like extreme dedication and passion to me. I saw another neighbor who owns a massive collection of miniature model trains complete with miniature replica cities, cars, people, moving parts and pieces and small blinking stop lights. Amazing hobby, I thought. He must be passionate. My own husband, who has played golf his entire life, will play in extreme hot and cold temperatures. Why? He loves the game; that's his passion. Even my son's soccer coach volunteers his time unselfishly because he loves the sport and finds personal fulfillment in developing kids into young athletes. Passion at its best, I thought.

I learned that passion can be about anything. It can be a hobby, a sport, an activity, a way of living, anything that brings you personal enjoyment. It didn't take me long to find my passion. It was right in front of me—my family. I changed my priorities, including my career, family schedule, and personal goals. I quit my full-time job and started my own marketing and media consulting firm. I worked out of my home to be closer to my family. Owning and working at my own business also meant that I had more control over my schedule. I carved out time to attend my kids' school and sporting events. I had time to volunteer in my community and take time for myself, including a monthly ninety-minute massage. During the first couple of years, I grew the business into a successful niche agency specializing in health care, physician, and non-profit marketing. I achieved all the business success I was willing to manage.

More recently, I refined my passion pursuit even further. I decided to move away from the agency business and morph into the information business. I began a public speaking career, which allows me to share my nearly twenty years of professional marketing and public relations experience with small business owners across the country and around the world. I also decided to address a burning desire inside of me of wanting to write a book. As a journalism major in college, writing has always been a fundamental passion at my core. Every job I have ever had has been in communications with writing a key component. My desire to change my business model stems from my passion to feel less stressed, have more family time, write, speak, educate, and inform.

I now spend my days speaking on this topic and on small business marketing, writing my book, and most recently writing a new blog, which by the way, is the result of asking myself a passionate, *What if?* question. I'll explain. Recently I watched the movie, *Julie & Julia*, about a woman who blogged her way through her experiences cooking Julia Child's published recipes. I asked myself, what if I was my own Julie and Julia? What if I were to blog about the ideas I'm including in my book? What if I could show the world that these ideas work by using them in my own business and document my progress in a blog? What if... well...I launched the blog without an additional thought. I now share my business marketing journey with the world. I've opened my "marketing toolbox," and I am utilizing all of the no cost/low cost ideas that I can think of to market my own business as well as sharing insights, tips, and how-to's for other business owners.

It's exciting to wake up every day just to see who has commented on the previous day's blog posting. It's a complete departure from the way I was accustomed to working. It has forced me to rethink how I work, when I work, and why I work in the first place. The result is I don't do anything that is not in line with my pursuit of my passions. The blogging experience is an entirely different way of pursuing my passion for writing. I am having more fun working than I have had in the past twenty years of my career. I feel more creative, relaxed, confident, and occasionally a little silly both at work and at play with my family. Because I've re-prioritized my life around my ultimate passion, my family, I now experience more personal satisfaction and happiness than ever before. I have rediscovered peace and laughter.

True, or what is known as magnetic, north is what navigators use to adjust their course of flight to ensure they reach their destination. If you feel you are off course, you need to adjust your compass to your true north and get back on the passion pursuit track. But how exactly do you find true north in your life? It's been my experience that the process of re-prioritizing my life and adjusting my internal compass direction involved five components. If you want to achieve your dreams and feel fulfilled in the process, you need to find the courage within you to make tough decisions. Then consider following in my footsteps:

Know Thyself and Thy Purpose

Most business owners write down their business goals, but how many of us take the time to write down our life goals? If you want to be different than you are or do something different with your life, I dare you to write your goals, desires, or dreams on a piece of paper. Think I'm crazy? Think again. Once I wrote my goals on paper, I became more dedicated to achieving them. I was suddenly committed to the pursuit of passion—how great does that sound?

Discover Your Hidden Passion

What do you love to do? What do you want to learn? Ask yourself, *What if?* What have you always thought about doing but didn't have the courage, strength, or determination to do? Your passion might be a hobby, a sport, playing an instrument or it might be the kind of work you do or the way you do your work. Maybe it's spending time with your children and family. Maybe it's a hobby like sewing, woodworking, or painting. Your individual passion pursuit should be what gives you energy and enthusiasm for life. It should be what fuels your imagination every day and inspires you to endure whatever life hands you.

Welcome Change and Invite Passion

Anthony Robbins said, "If you do what you've always done, you'll get what you've always gotten." If you want to change your life in any way, I've found the best way to begin is to pick one small thing each week to change and then do it. With fifty-two weeks in a year, you can easily change fifty-two small things and live a completely different life by this time next year! The changes could also be invitations—simple ways to start bringing your passions into your life daily, weekly, or monthly. I've been doing this for the past year and by making room in my life for new pursuits, I've had to dismiss old baggage, habits, and fears. It's been a freeing experience. Inviting new passion into your life also makes it real. It becomes easier because your desires and dreams begin to materialize as they enter your comfort zone in a more permanent way.

Identify your Destination

Don't leave your dreams to chance. Plan what your life will look like in the next ninety days, six months, one year, three years, five years, or more. What will you be doing? Who will be with you? How much money will you have? Where will you live? How will you spend your days? What will you be doing to bring more fun, adventure, and fulfillment into your life? I did this exercise two years ago and I'm still working toward my timeline. I envisioned myself being self-employed, being more available to my family, living a stress-free and financially secure life, becoming a professional speaker and author, and achieving unimaginable success. This would allow me to travel the world and visit Hawaii at least once a year where I could sit on a secluded beach with a coconut umbrella drink and write 'til sunset. I have a vivid imagination and very colorful expectations of what I want my life to become. I have achieved most of what I envisioned in less than two years. Now I'm focusing on a longer term plan with more lofty goals. Try to imagine and visualize yourself as the person you wish to become. That's your destination.

Jumping into the Passion Pool

Like Nike, it's time to just do it. All the planning, thinking, and good intentions won't make your passion pursuit any easier unless you take action. If you wish to make a change in your life and see your dreams and desires come true, you need to act on your plan. For some, this means jumping in cold turkey—all or nothing—taking a risk and living La Vida Loca! For others who aren't so daring, there's another option. Because most of us balance obligation with pursuit of passion, a more comfortable way to begin is to ease your way into it. Think of a swimming pool. There's a deep end for those wanting to dive in head first and then there's the shallow end for those who want to test the waters. I chose to ease into my passion pursuit because it allowed me to enter the passion pool and dabble while I completed other things and put some of my obligations to rest. It also gave me the opportunity to gradually experience the benefits of pursuing my passion. You might not be ready to jump in over your head, but there's nothing preventing you from testing the water with a pinky toe or splashing in the shallow end for a little while.

To find my true north, I had to focus all of my attention in the direction of my goals, desires, and dreams in an effort to attract the success I wished to have in my life. It was as much about knowing what I did not want as it was about knowing what I did want. Now whenever I get that uneasy, unfulfilled feeling, I make the time to nurture that place inside of me that drives my zest for adventure; that place where all my creativity is generated; where my talents, desires, and passions converge with action. I regularly review these steps and make adjustments to my plan along the way.

Don't let anyone try to convince you that pursuing your passion is not practical or worth the time, money, or effort. It might sound totally ridiculous to others. Who cares? Passion is sometimes risky, but it is what brings value and meaning to our lives. I consider naysayers to be people who haven't discovered their own passions yet and who haven't awakened to the benefits we are experiencing. I've learned that the quality of my life is better when I pursue my desires and dreams. I am a better wife, a better mother, and a better person because of it. Find your true north by adjusting your internal compass and fearlessly pursuing your life's passions. With so much at stake, doesn't it almost seem unreasonable not to relentlessly pursue your passion? Life is too fragile not to enjoy doing what you love with the people you love the most. After all, isn't that the ultimate passion?

About the Author

Cheryl Smith is a professional marketing and media executive who specializes in working with small- and medium- sized businesses to develop their brands on shoestring budgets. As a professional speaker and coach, her audiences and clients enjoy well-researched material filled with practical solutions.

In 2005, Cheryl founded Banyan Communications Group, LLC, a niche consulting firm specializing in business marketing and public relations. Her insight into the ever-changing marketing landscape is built upon her personal experiences. Her career began in professional journalism writing for *United Press International* and the Peoria *Journal Star*. She later was the director of marketing and media spokesperson for six hospitals and several health care companies including Evangelical Health Systems; Advocate Health Care in Chicago; and HCA Sunrise Health in Las Vegas.

Cheryl holds a Master of Arts in public affairs reporting from the University of Illinois, a Bachelor of Arts in mass communication/print journalism from Western Illinois University, is a trained facilitator and affiliate member of the National Speakers Association, Las Vegas Chapter.

She is presently pursuing her passion for writing by authoring a book on small business marketing. She also writes a blog, "Small Business Marketing Miser Advisor," in which she offers tips and marketing how-to's for small businesses.

Cheryl Smith may be contacted via:
Banyan Communications Group, LLC
PO Box 34325 Las Vegas, NV 89133
(702) 505-6446
www.cherylsmithspeaker.com
csmith@cherylsmithspeaker.com

Becoming Marilyn

LAURA PETERS

"How did you become Marilyn Monroe?"

"How does someone get a job like that?"

I have been asked these questions thousands of times over the years when I performed as Marilyn in the famous *Legends in Concert* show at the Imperial Palace in Las Vegas.

For as long as I can remember, I wanted to be an actress. I don't recall ever deciding I wanted to be one or a moment when I thought *that's what I want to be*. I just always knew that's what I *was*...an actress. But there were some big challenges I had to overcome. I was painfully shy in public and had little self-confidence. Being born an actress came with a price. My parents referred to me as the "dramatic" child, the one who gave the rest of the family something to talk about, accused of exaggerating, just because I told a story with flair. My sisters protested, "Don't believe her; she's acting!" I thought these were good things, though it was quite clear my family didn't always think so. I couldn't change who I was nor did I want to. I became part of the drama department in high school. I felt very comfortable there, a sense of belonging, though I wasn't secure enough to handle the label of "drama freak" used by the other kids at school to taunt us. I was an actress, but I also wanted to be "cool."

In college, I decided to major in dramatic arts. Grossmont College was a small two-year college that launched the careers of many who eventually worked their way into the theater and movies and just happened to be the local junior college. My neighbor was an English professor at the college who warned me not to get my hopes up and think

I could actually get a role in one their productions. "That department is a 'clique.' You don't just get in. You have to earn your place ; 'they' have to get to know you." Yet, I got the lead understudy role with my first audition for "The Wager," which meant that I performed the matinee shows, and should the lead actress meet with an untimely accident or death, I would be ready to step in. For my second audition, I won the starring role as Marcelle in the French farce-comedy, "Hotel Paradiso."

I determined the rules which apply to other people don't always apply to me...an idea which keeps getting reinforced as I go through life. This is also when I met the director, Clark Mires. He was the first person in the industry who believed I was talented, funny, and even called me "clever." When Clark was interviewed by a reporter who was doing a story on the production, he said that I had a natural sense of comedic timing. I thought he was crazy! Rarely was I on time for a rehearsal, or for that matter, anything else. Later, I found out he meant I was funny. No one had ever said I was funny or used the adjective "clever" when describing me. I loved him for that. It gave me validation and confidence. Finally someone besides me believed in my talent.

When creating my role as Marilyn Monroe, I ran across an interview of Shelly Winters talking about being roommates with the real Marilyn when they both were starting out in Hollywood before they became famous. Shelly asked Marilyn, "If a thousand agents and directors out there said you have no talent and you'll never make in this business, what would you do?" Marilyn said in a soft and definite voice, "Then a thousand agents and directors would be wrong." She knew who she was. She created Marilyn and no one could tell her any different. She believed in herself. She became independent of the "good opinions of others." This characteristic of hers helped me become the person I wanted to be and helped me achieve my dreams and goals.

The real world didn't give me any time to pursue my dream of being an actress. I became pregnant at seventeen and a mother of an active little boy at the age of eighteen. Job, college, baby, it was all overwhelming for me and I thought "something's got to give." So I kept the job and the baby. I didn't give up the dream, just the hope of it becoming real. I was a single mom; I had to be responsible and get a real job. Thus began a series of jobs, none that lasted a long time, just long enough to pay the bills and be a responsible parent.

In 1983, a girlfriend heard a radio advertisement that the airline PSA was offering round trip tickets to Las Vegas for only $50. She said, "Let's go for the weekend. It'll be fun and we'll meet rich men." She had it all planned. We'd share a room at the Hilton for only $20 a night and we would eat shrimp cocktails—they were only a dollar. I'd never been to Las Vegas; well, not really. On spring break from high school, my family took a vacation and drove through Las Vegas. My dad parked our camper in the Circus Circus parking lot. My sisters and I played cards and listened to our transistor radios in the camper while my parents went inside. That doesn't actually count. Going to Las Vegas for the weekend sounded exciting, adventurous, frivolous, and irresponsible, so I said "Yes!"

After less than five hours in Las Vegas and three shrimp cocktails later, my girlfriend was nowhere to be found. I never wanted to eat shrimp again, and I found out that playing blackjack at the tables with real money in Las Vegas wasn't the same as playing in the camper with matches. I lost my whole gambling budget of twenty dollars in less than twenty minutes, so I left. I went to the center bar, ordered a champagne cocktail, and proceeded to sulk. Las Vegas wasn't turning out to be the whirlwind adventure I had thought it would be.

A man took a seat next to me and started talking, as though he knew me. He said he got tired of playing keno and thought he'd come say hello. Then he asked, "So, how's the show going?"

I replied, "Who do you think I am and what show?"

A bit taken aback, he said, "Aren't you Susan, the Marilyn in *Legends*?"

I had no idea what he was talking about. "My name is Laura," I said.

He looked at me—surprised—and asked, "Has anyone ever told you that you look like Marilyn Monroe?" I may have heard it once or twice, but I never thought anything of it. Then he introduced himself. "Hi, I'm Bernie Allen." He was a comedian in town and was once a part of the comedy team, Allen and Rossi. He continued; "Well, if you're not in the show, you ought to be."

I thought, "*Wow; a famous comedian in Las Vegas thinks I look like Marilyn Monroe and that I should be in a show.*" I don't know which thrilled me the most...the compliment or that looking like Marilyn could get me in a show. When I told Bernie that my dream was to be an actress, he called John Stuart, the producer of *Legends In Concert,* a new live tribute show in Las Vegas at the Imperial Palace, with performers who not only looked like Buddy Holly, Elvis Presley, Judy Garland, and Marilyn Monroe, but also danced with a live orchestra and sang, using their own voices. John met me the next day and gave me a comp to see the show that night, which was great and the performers were amazing. I knew that's what I was going to do.

John Stuart told me I had a "good look" and asked if I could sing. I told him yes, I knew all of Marilyn's songs. This wasn't true; I had no idea what Marilyn sang, how she sounded, or what movies she did. I left out the part that my singing career didn't exist beyond my shower. But hey! I was an actress; I knew I could do it. He said I needed to lose about twenty pounds, which really stunned me; no one had ever told me I was fat before. We exchanged contact information and he told me to keep in touch.

I took that literally. I flew back to San Diego and proceeded to research everything I could on Marilyn Monroe. I watched her movies, mimicked her voice, learned her songs, and studied every movement she made. It became my second job. I called John Stuart every month. I've been asked where that persistence came from. I said, "What persistence? He told me to keep in touch."

Not long after that I lost my day job, I was getting evicted from my apartment because I couldn't afford the rent, and my 1972 Pinto was barely running. I sold just about everything I owned and moved in with my sister. I told my dad this was my chance to move to Los Angeles and start my career as an actress. He gave me lecture #1257 on why this was the craziest idea I'd ever come up with, how totally irresponsible it was, and asked how in the world did I ever think I could make a living being an actress when there were a hundred thousand other girls prettier and more talented than me trying to do the same thing. This was my dad's loving way of trying to talk sense into me. It hurt; I wanted the approval of my family, my parents—especially my dad. They didn't see me the way I saw myself. I knew I would never be happy living the life they wanted for me. It was hard, but that's when I started divorcing myself from needing their emotional support and approval. I just kept thinking what Marilyn said...*they were wrong*. When I got to LA, I found out my dad was wrong. There weren't a hundred thousand girls; there were millions, or at least it seemed like it. I was armed with the best blessings I could have possessed: persistence and ignorance. I had no idea how I was going to do it, but not achieving my goal was never an option. I didn't have a plan B. I signed up with Ron Smith look-a-likes; I was befriended by a photographer, Jimmy, who worked with Ron. He took hundreds of pictures of me as Marilyn. I started getting paying gigs right away. Singing happy birthday at parties and doing photo shoots here and there didn't always pay all the bills, so I also got a day job...several of them in fact. I was a bank teller for a short time when I was told very politely that I'd be better suited in another profession, as in anything other than banking. I was a receptionist for a famous vocal coach, who helped me perfect Marilyn's voice, and a PBX operator for a huge law firm in Beverly Hills. That job gave me the ability to continue to call John Stuart every month without having to pay long distant charges. I told him about the twenty pounds I had lost and all the experience I was getting performing as Marilyn. Then one hot July day in 1984, when I was answering and directing calls, a voice said, "Laura, is that you?" John Stuart was calling me. He had put together a second *Legends In Concert* show to perform at the Hollywood Palladium during the summer Olympics. He had hired a New York actress to play Marilyn and she ditched the show for a bit part on TV. He needed a Marilyn right away and wanted me to audition.

When I got home my roommate informed me that two agents had called and left messages; I had two separate auditions scheduled for a Marilyn part the next day. Both were at the same place where I was meeting John Stuart. I thought, great! I'd have more time to prove myself.

I showed up with my best Marilyn on, but my stomach was turning so fast I thought I was going to throw up. I was escorted to a room backstage that had been curtained off with just a small table and two chairs. I thought it was kind of odd I was the only one there. Usually there would be twenty or more girls waiting when I went to auditions. Johnny came and reintroduced himself to me and commented on how good I looked; no mention of the "twenty pounds." He asked if I could sing and if I knew Marilyn's songs. I said yes to both and started to name all her songs I knew. He asked me to sing "I Wanna Be Loved By You," so I did. By now I wasn't even nervous; I was accustomed to singing a cappella. I really never sang any other way. He said I sounded good and he liked what he saw. He then said he was auditioning a couple of other girls and would get back with me by that evening. That's when I found myself in a bit of an awkward position; how was I going to tell him that I was his next two auditions? I asked him if one of those auditions was at one o'clock sent by a local agency. He said, "Yes." I was a bit hesitant when I told him that it was me he was to audition. He looked surprised and then started laughing. This gave me some relief. He then said, "Okay, I guess I only have one other audition this afternoon." I looked at him and asked if that would be at two o'clock with another local agency. After a moment he got this astonished look on his face. He said, "Wait a minute; I'm supposed to audition three Marilyns today and all three are *you*?" I just shook my head yes, realizing that I definitely should have mentioned this up front, until...he burst out laughing. It was the only time I ever saw John Stuart at a loss for words. He said, "Honey, you've got the biggest balls I've ever run across in this business." I got the part.

The next day I was driven to the Hollywood Palladium and escorted to my dressing room where I was told to "get ready." I felt like a movie star. I wasn't nervous at all; it felt so familiar, even though it wasn't. I had performed onstage before, but not for an audience of this size. I had never sung for people who were actually paying attention and never with live music, let alone a whole orchestra. Up until now, the only microphone I ever held and sang into was my hairbrush. I sang, "I Wanna Be Loved By You," and "Diamonds Are A Girl's Best Friend." I had no idea what the band was playing; they were loud and definitely were not playing in the same key in which I was singing. The audience applauded, though I have no idea why. It was awful, I was awful, but I was having so much fun I couldn't stop smiling. Maybe they were applauding out of sympathy. *That poor thing up there; what does she think she's doing?*

After the show, Johnny came up to me and said, "Honey, I think we should have a rehearsal tomorrow with you and the band." I just looked at him and asked, "You think?" The show at the Palladium was only for a short engagement, but it was the most exciting two weeks of my life. All I could think about was starring in the show all the time in Las Vegas.

About a year later, John Stuart called and asked me to audition for the show in Las Vegas. By now, I had much more experience and singing lessons. I flew to Las Vegas for the second time; this time to audition for the show where two years before I had sat in the audience in awe of the talent and with the hope that I could be part of it one day. After the audition, Johnny came up and asked me, "So, how does it feel to be a headliner in a Las Vegas show?" This time it was I who was at a loss for words. That night as I was lying in bed in my hotel room trying to digest all that had happened, I remember thinking, *so this is what it feels like to win the lottery; this is what it feels like when your big dreams come true.*

How did I become Marilyn Monroe in a Las Vegas show? By pursuing my passion and believing in myself.

About the Author

 Laura Peters is a professional speaker, performer and entertainer who has been in the industry for more than 30 years. She is best known for her portrayal as Marilyn Monroe in the world famous Las Vegas *Legends in Concert* show. She headlined on the Las Vegas strip as well as toured all over the world. Her one woman show, *Becoming Marilyn*, is scheduled to open in the fall. The show is a musical...sometimes serious...comedy, on the parallels and differences of the woman who portrayed Marilyn and the woman who was Marilyn. An exploration of the "what if's" for both women had Marilyn not passed away at the age of thirty-six.

Laura is an affiliate member of the National Speakers Association, Las Vegas chapter. With an upbeat, informative, and entertaining style, her expertise is in the area of helping professional sales teams increase their productivity and achieve their goals. She is passionate about assisting others on their path to achieving their dreams, desires, and goals.

Laura lives in Las Vegas with her fiancé, Kevin Thornton. She has two children and four grandchildren.

Laura Peters may be contacted via:
(702) 378-4338
lauragpeters@aol.com
www.kre8inc.com
www.voiceoveractress.com

Choose Passion

JUDI MOREO

"You can have anything you want if you want it desperately enough. You must want it with an inner exuberance that erupts through the skin and joins the energy that created the world."

Sheilah Graham, American Gossip Columnist

Passion is the fuel that drives us to accomplish our goals. If your tank is full of passion, you are going to go a long way. Passion comes when we believe in something, when our purpose is clear.

What gets you excited? What do you love? What do you feel strongly about in your life? What would you do even if you didn't get paid? What are your special talents? How do you know when something is right? Have you tried to do something that you've never done before? What do you secretly wish you could do? How badly do you want to do it?

Listen to your heart to find what it is you want to do and what you feel passionate about. Put your entire focus into it, rather than just getting up, getting dressed, going to work, and getting through the day. When you are excited about life, you'll get up early, be on time, do your best, give more than is expected, and be happy doing it. If you don't feel this, perhaps you need to make some changes. If your job isn't as satisfying as you would like, maybe you need a new job. Perhaps it won't pay as much or won't have the perks your current job has, but when you condition your mind, it will change the condition of your life. The money will come when you love what you do and have enthusiasm for it.

Many of us think we have no control over our lives. Failure to accomplish what we want in life is a result of failing to believe in ourselves enough. We let doubt sneak in and then we make excuses about

169

our abilities, time constraints, training and talents. Doubt creates stress, panic, and anxiety. These defeat our plans and goals.

Sometimes people succeed in a conventional sense, but lack happiness because they aren't doing what they really want. Instead, they attempt to fulfill the desires and goals of someone else rather than their own. Perhaps they have fallen under the influence of a parent or a spouse. How can they feel passionate about something they don't really want? They have probably even stopped making any effort toward their real goals, because of a fear of failure, a fear of rejection, or a lack of self-worth. If only they would pursue their own interests and use their natural talents, they would be sure to succeed.

If you are willing to accept a job you don't like, one that creates stress, but pays well, then you must be willing to pay the price, and the price you pay is a lack of passion and joy. Many of us have been taught from childhood that it is selfish and self-centered to be happy in what we do. We've been taught we must work hard to get ahead. If we can learn to work passionately, we will go further than hard work will ever take us.

Many of us are very good at keeping commitments to other people, but not the ones we make to ourselves. We put everyone else's priorities ahead of our own. We make promises to ourselves that we don't keep. We have excuses such as I was too busy, my boss needed me, I had to go to the children's school function, my husband needed it done for him, and all the while that little voice inside of us says, "What about me? Don't I deserve some attention as well?" When we don't keep the commitments we make to ourselves, we feel hurt, frustrated, resentful, unworthy, and our passion dies.

What could your passion do if only you would unleash it? Passion is like the wind in our sails. It pushes us in the direction we want to go. Without passion, we might never leave the harbor. If we allow our passion to die, we might end up on the rocks or stuck in the doldrums of mediocrity.

If you keep doing the same old thing in the same old way...only harder and longer, you are going to get the same old results and you are going to hate it. Life treats you as you treat life. In order to be passionate about life, you may have to undergo a mind change. You may need to re-evaluate what's really important to you. As you observe your life and the lives of others, you might see that living a life without passion is a costly compromise. It is much easier to live a life of passion than it is to live a stressful, unhealthy, unfulfilling, though well paid existence.

When we know what we want and take action in the direction of our goals, it gives us a reason to get up in the morning. When the goal is our own and we work toward it, we have more energy and our days become exciting.

Think about how much time you have left to live, if you live to the average life expectancy, which is about 77 years. How old are you now? How much time do you have left to finally live your life the way you want to live? We are all born into greatness and through our upbringing or life circumstances, we sometimes allow life to pull us down into mediocrity. It's not necessary. Decide now how you want to spend your time. If you are feeling like life is passing you by and you don't feel a burning passion inside of you urging you to fulfill your life's purpose, then something is wrong.

When we have passion, our minds let go of blocks and barriers, because we are focused on what we wish to accomplish and the expectation of what good we can make happen. When we are passionate, we take great joy in our steps forward – both big and small, using what didn't work as lessons learned, setting new goals, moving onward and upward to achieve these new goals. In other words, when we are passionate, we get on with it!

Passionate people are enthusiastic people. The word *enthusiasm* comes from the Greek words, *en theos*, which mean "the spirit within." We each need to unleash the spirit that is within us. You can't expect other people to get excited about your ideas or projects if you aren't excited. If you don't have a tone of enthusiasm in your voice, people won't buy into your ideas. If you can focus your enthusiasm toward achieving your goals, others will want to help you achieve them.

When I started my first business, I had a total of $2,000.00 in my savings account. I found a small office to rent, paid a security deposit, as well as my first and last month's rent. After buying my office furniture and the supplies I needed to run my business, I didn't have any money left, but I was passionate. The first day of the second month came and the rent was due. I visited my landlord and told him I didn't have the money to pay the rent. I asked him to allow me credit for a month. I was sure I would make the needed amount in a few days. He looked at me and said, "The man next door bet me you wouldn't last in business six months. I bet him you would. If you can hang in there for six months, I'll make enough money on the bet to cover your rent. Do you think you can hang in there?" I'm not sure if it was his betting on me or the other guy betting against me that fueled my passion that day. Maybe it was both. I was even more determined to be successful.

I was so enthusiastic about my goal and believed in my dream enough that I pursued my passion with a vengeance. It may have been a rough start, but it wasn't long until Universal Models was the finest modeling school and the biggest model agency in the Southwest. I ran an extremely well known and profitable business for 17 years. I even received a Las Vegas Chamber of Commerce "Woman of Achievement" award.

You may be thinking, "Well, that was you…and that was then. Things were easier then." Excuse me. Things were never easy. In fact, things were often very hard, and very stressful, but I was happy. Your next question might be, "How can we be happy and passionate every day when we are dealing with the stresses of life?"

Your world is what you make it, through your thoughts, words, and attitudes. Focus on the positives and stop worrying. Worry simply strangles our creative abilities and keeps us from being able to look for solutions and new ways of doing things. Your brain knows how to think and if allowed, it will create the right things to do and say. Most of us don't take the time to think. We don't spend time alone in the quiet. If we are alone, we usually have the television or the radio blaring, forcing our brains to work at taking in information rather than doing what it needs to do. We need to listen to our inner voices. Turn off the television and the radio for at least 20 minutes a day and spend that time in silence by yourself. Put positive thoughts into your head. Your subconscious doesn't care what you put into it. It will respond to any thought it receives. Focus on your biggest goal and mentally see yourself achieving it or having it. When you program your mind with positive thoughts, you realign your body chemistry and make yourself healthier and happier. When you think and behave in a positive manner, you not only cause others to enjoy the experience of being around you, you keep yourself energetic and make your own life more exciting.

When you are passionate and you act purposefully, you are putting faith into action, going after your goals, and doing something that makes life better for yourself or others. When you put your faith into action, you are giving up uncertainty, doubt, and fear. When I started Universal Models with only $2,000.00, I knew in my heart that I would be successful. I was passionate about my dream. Uncertainty, doubt, and fear never entered my mind. I knew the city of Las Vegas needed a legitimate model agency and I was positive I could make that happen. I knew conventions needed dependable personnel who could work in the exhibits as sales people, hostesses, receptionists and spokespersons. I knew that movies filmed in Las Vegas would need "extras." Most of all, I knew I could organize these things well. I did it all...and more. I loved my business and the people with whom I dealt.

When you feel like you brought something to a successful conclusion, made good use of your time, and marked another item off your "to do" list, you boost your self-esteem and your self-confidence and you add even more fuel to your passion. After all, if you did that, you can do more.

Alfred Lord Tennyson once said, "The happiness of a man in this life does not consist in the absence of but in the mastery of his passions."

Passion is an integral part of achieving success. People with passion have a sense of purpose and meaning. They are achieving things. They don't waste their time. If you feel strongly enough about something, you will put your effort and time toward it. You will be passionate and you will make your dreams come to life. If you don't feel strongly about something, it won't matter to you if it ever gets done or if anything changes.

Success is not an accident. Successful people make themselves successful. They have goals, dreams, desires, wants, needs, and passion. They develop an attitude that attracts success. When passionate people are asked how they are doing, they reply, "Wonderful,""Marvelous," or "Terrific." They are in pursuit of the realization of their dreams. They don't have time to complain, or be negative. There's an old saying, "Little people talk about other people. Average people talk about things. Great people talk about ideas and possibilities." Passionate people also talk about ideas and possibilities. Maybe that's why so many of them become known as "great."

Malcolm Forbes, publisher of *Forbes Magazine*, is quoted as saying, "Your adrenaline has to run. If you don't feel exhilarated by achieving your objectives and excelling at what you are doing, then you'll never do much very well." Do you know what makes your adrenaline run?

Dare to be passionate about your relationships, your values, your beliefs, and your job. Passion is like a magnet. It attracts the things and people we want in our lives. Passion energizes us and helps us overcome fear. When we are passionate, we experience higher levels of joy, love, and satisfaction.

Your goals have more chance of becoming reality when you go after them with passion. Many people talk about how committed they are, but when push comes to shove, they quit. They don't have passion. Real passion doesn't give up until the desired result is achieved. Even when an obstacle gets in your way or you have a setback, you never give up. Passionate people understand there is a price to pay to achieve anything worthwhile.

Go after what you want with passion! Find out the risks and rewards before you decide to follow a particular path. If we take the time to think about what possible obstacles will come up, we can be prepared to take alternative action. Be prepared by asking yourself, "How would I handle this situation if I run into a roadblock or if an emergency occurs?" No matter what your situation, you can make your journey easier if you prepare yourself by exploring the alternative routes in advance.

Don't underestimate yourself and overestimate others. You are not inferior to anyone. Put all your effort into what you do. Do more than is required. Do it to the best of your ability. Turn off any negative or doubtful voices in your head and listen only to the sound of that little train from the children's book. It said, "I think I can. I think I can. I think I can." Think you can. If you think you can, you will.

Life is an adventure to be lived. Today is a new beginning. Imagine the exciting things you can do, the wonderful relationships you can have, the places you can go, and who you can be when you give up the fear and live your life with passion.

About The Author

Judi Moreo, CSP, is the author of *You Are More Than Enough: Every Woman's Guide to Purpose, Passion, and Power,* and its companion, Achievement Journal. She is an award-winning businesswoman and motivational speaker. Her superb talent for customizing programs to meet organizational needs has gained her a prestigious following around the world. Her passion for living an extraordinary life is mirrored in her zeal for helping others realize their potential and achieve their goals. With her dynamic personality and style, she is an unforgettable speaker, inspiring motivator, and an exceptional coach.

Judi Moreo may be contacted via:
judi@judimoreo.com
www.judimoreo.com
www.youaremorethanenough.com
Turning Point International
P. O. Box 231360,
Las Vegas, NV 89105
(702) 896-2228

uture

There is no end. There is no beginning. There is only the passion of life.

—Federico Fellini

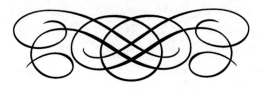

The Muses Whisper

SANDRA GORE NIELSEN

When a man is willing and eager, the gods join in.
~ Aeschylus 500 B.C.

The gods gave me a gift. I stumbled along most of my life not knowing I had it. I followed one path, and then another, looking back on my youth as the golden time, and looking at my golden years as, *Is this it? Is the best over? Do I just wait to die?*

Then at a time when most people retire, I stumbled on my gift impatiently waiting for me to be ready. In a perfect world, I would have spent my life developing my craft, honing it, practicing it for 10,000 hours. But I was too busy living to let my spirit soar and my imagination run wild. I wasn't ready.

In his book, *Outliers: The Story of Success*, the author, Malcolm Gladwell, claims there's a 10,000 hour rule…a magic number of practice hours needed to master any skill. To get to mastery level fast, I needed to start as soon as possible and work as many hours as possible.

I didn't find writing until late, so I had to make up for lost time. I'm not complaining. I had a few other passions I worked through before I got to this one. Each of those passions, some more fervent than others, led me to the day I dared to call myself an author. And each of my passions, past and present, inspires my stories.

"What is there left that you want to do with your life?" my friend Barb asked.

"I want to write a book." I thought my words came out of nowhere, but now I know the Muses whispered.

I set a clear and attainable goal: Put words on paper and bind paper in cover. Voila! A book! That goal is already outdated with eBooks. You can skip the whole bind-in-cover part, unless like me, you love to touch.

The criterion for my first book was quite simple: it had to be fast. I didn't want to be overwhelmed by research, scared off in the beginning, or get bogged down halfway. I needed the jump-start confidence of finishing quickly. *I did it. It can be done—and by me.*

The greatest hurdle was to allow myself to say, "I am a writer." It took some chutzpah. Who was I to write a book? People study or write articles for years before they dare. They enter hundreds of contests for short stories and enroll in workshops and writers groups. I skipped all that. I didn't have time. I did keep in mind what brilliant Greeks said 2500 years ago: *Be what you wish to seem.* They listened well to the Muses. They built temples to them.

Part of the same process was acceptance. I was not writing for a Pulitzer Prize. I came to terms that my book would not be great literature and not a bestseller—although one always hopes! I had to get over the deadliest of thresholds: "Nobody reads. Who needs another book?" But who cares about that? I faced the limitations and plunged in. I was doing it for me. Don't I deserve fulfillment?

You get to your passion on a winding path, and each step, even the missteps, have a purpose. Your whole life is linked. I wanted to be a speaker, someone with the gift of blarney who stands up in front of groups and gets paid to talk. I've always been a good talker—some say too much.

Thinking I had found something to be passionate about again, I joined the National Speaker's Association and hung around like a groupie. When asked what I spoke about, my pat response was, "I'm searching for my message." What I was really saying was that the Muses were mute.

I saw that most successful speakers have a book. A book was the needed credential to be taken seriously. A book is the best business card you'll ever have. My conclusion? Write the book first; that seemed the hardest part. Then talk about it.

Writing an informational book requires you have information that is useful to others. The recession had hit. I was feeling the pinch and spending my Saturdays digging through junk to find treasures at swap meets and antique malls. The glory days were over for a while, but I still needed the thrill of new stuff in my life. What could be easier for me than writing a book on shopping for quality at rock bottom prices?

Feedback stunned me. I found out there are women who won't wear anything that ever belonged to a stranger, as if a secondhand mink carried the plague. I couldn't believe anyone could be that dumb in today's economy.

I suddenly had something to say that might help people. "Shopping is Zen!" "Don't feel you are less, feel you are more." "You'll find exactly what the universe knows you need." I also had a theory about female psychology. *Shopping is to women what sex is to men.* They can never get enough. If there's one thing I understand, it's insatiable need.

The book became an obsession. I hadn't felt such gut-wrenching passion since the days I travelled like a gypsy without possessions or responsibilities. Not even the bloodbath of my righteous political years could compare.

How did I know writing would be my passion? I didn't until I sat down and tried. The further I got into my book, the more I realized it was the writing that fired me up, not the speaking. The words flowed from my imagination through my fingers into the keyboard. I taught myself Photoshop and struggled with Adobe InDesign until tears flowed and I wanted to pitch my laptop from the balcony. I wasn't being paid. In fact, it was costing me. I persisted because I was driven—yes, delightfully and compulsively *driven.* I had no choice but to do what I was doing. How wonderful to feel that again!

When I held my first book in my hands, one that I created from cover to cover—all the writing, photography and artwork—I felt something akin to childbirth. Being completely honest and asking forgiveness from my family, I think it was almost (I said *almost*) better.

Once set on the path, there was more to come. While writing my shopping book, Judi Moreo invited me to contribute to the first *Life Choices* anthology, *Navigating Difficult Paths.* I anguished. I was being self-indulgent. My life had been smooth sailing compared to other acts of courage. Who was I to talk about a life choice? I thought of a thousand reasons not to do it, including I was selfish and just plain *not good enough*.

In the end, I couldn't turn down any chance to be published. My memoir piece, "A True Love Story" is short and shamelessly romantic with an important message: Don't waste any time if you know what you want. Put on the blinders and go!

Next, I took the scariest leap there is in writing. I tried writing fiction. I invented a story from a blank page. From the first moment I stepped back in time to live Isis in ancient Egypt, I knew writing fiction was my passion with a capital P.

How did I know? When you're pursuing your passion, you don't have to ask. You welcome every day as an opportunity to do more. You arrange your life to minimize distractions. You don't allow yourself to get side-tracked. You don't neglect your family, but you don't put them first anymore, except at holidays and in emergencies. You stop obsessing on their happiness or lack of, and instead obsess on what you want to accomplish.

I have yet another theory—yes, I'm full of them. No artist or person of accomplishment ever achieved anything without being an egoist, maybe even an egotist. You've got to believe that what you want to do with your life is the most important thing. If you don't believe that, you'll never live your passion. You'll just dream about it.

The practical start to my writing began with my blog "SandraOfftheStrip.com" inspired by a Las Vegas workshop with Steve Pavlina. "Off the Strip" covers a lot of territory; it includes any place in the universe—physical, mental or spiritual. I had free rein to express my views on any topic.

I went all the way back to my childhood to rediscover my fantasy; it had always been there. A passionate daydreamer, I lulled myself to sleep with stories I invented about being kidnapped by pirates or Vikings. It was not a huge leap to romantic historical adventure novels.

Writing a novel does take a lot of work, only I never feel it much. When the Muses sing, there is no higher note. My metabolism speeds and I even sweat. It's an emotional roller coaster ride, so be warned. The Buddhist path of moderation doesn't work when you're living in a virtual world that is only interesting to others if loaded with drama. The more drama, the better.

The joy of writing is in the high points; I have to live with the lows when my story ends up in a box canyon—or when I finish the last line and sob because the characters are no more. I invented them; I coddled them; I tortured them. I even fell in love with them. They were alive and then they were dead. I solved that depression by writing sequels, so my characters keep acting out new material and blowing my mind. I love it when they surprise me. That's when the real fun begins.

I know I've hit my stride when the story is my first thought in the morning and my last thought at night. If worries try to butt in, I quickly kick them out. "Sorry, world, you have to wait."

A friend asked me why I felt driven to write. Who cares why I'm driven? I'm just happy following the Muses. For years I wandered around lost in my life, not knowing what I was supposed to be doing. I attended weekend workshops with life coaches, making lists of goals and analyzing my psyche according to whatever formula that guru invented.

I am so happy to feel driven again. How wonderful it is to have "more ideas than time" instead of "time with no ideas." I'm not wasting a minute. I'm not thinking much about the future. Who knows what tomorrow will bring? Maybe a top agent will fall from the sky.

I listened to the whispers and am the author of a non-fiction book, two memoir pieces, and two novels. I think I can safely call that "pursuing my passion."

Listen! The Muses will whisper if you open your ears. See! Imagine yourself as your passion. Dare! We are beings in search of meaning. Passion is meaning to the nth degree. Follow! Your passion will take you where you need to go and the Muses will hold your hand.

About the Author

Born in Kansas City, Sandra is a baby boomer who escaped the prairie to explore the world while her friends were partying at college. She returned to the United States after 25 years in Europe, Africa, Central America and the Middle East, with a Danish husband, an art degree and speaking five languages.

Her writing career is new and started when most people retire. After a full life of family, business and politics, she drew on her love of history, languages, mysticism, food, shopping and romance to create *The Red Mirror* with Isis who travels back and forth between two worlds. She has completed the first two books of the Trilogy, *Isis* in Late Period Egypt and *Athena* in Ptolemaic Egypt, and is working on *Elektra* set in Roman Egypt.

Pursing Your Passion is the second *Life Choices* anthology for Sandra. "A True Love Story" was published in 2010 in *Navigating Difficult Paths*. Her first book *Sex and the Zen of Shopping: How to Live Rich by Shopping Smart*, both self-help for the spirit and how to for the practical, was published in 2010. She is slowly compiling a cookbook of her own recipes plus those of talented friends around the globe.

Sandra and her husband of 36 years divide their time between a California beach house and a Las Vegas condo. They have two children in their twenties, a boy and a girl. You can read more about Sandra and her life at www.sandragorenielsen.com.

Sandra Gore Nielsen may be contacted via:
www.sandragorenielsen.com

The Cameo of Your Life

ANNE DREYER

....You can be ravishing at 20
Charming at 40
Or
Be irresistible for the rest of your life!
Coco Chanel

This phrase has been my dictum for over 30 years. I have experienced the miracle first hand, of how women, from all walks of life, of any shape, size or age, can blossom exactly where they are planted. I truly believe that women are one of the perfect creations, and can live a life of purpose, if they use their God given talents. Utilizing these gifts can result in positive change, impact positively on the lives of others, and allow a person to become irresistible forever! My passionate driving force behind teaching and training women about *how* to become *irresistible* has been a journey in empowering myself while teaching others to empower themselves.

The beginning of my journey

I grew up in a small mining town, Klerksdorp, in colonial South Africa in the 1950s. I had a most wonderful and happy childhood. My father was my idol, and his gracious manners, instilled in him by my cultured grandmother of French Huguenot decent, were part of my upbringing—I learned by example!

My mother had a natural gift and talent for hospitality. There was often an extra place or two set at our dinner table for an unexpected guest, and she could always stretch the meal to feed them. She could dress on a shoe string, with the wonderful ability to mix and match a limited wardrobe to appear as if she had tons of clothes. She was always well-groomed and always a lady.

My school friends came from different backgrounds, from professional class families to laborers who lived in ghettos. We mixed and mingled and never judged by material wealth. Many have remained my friends for fifty years and my mothers' words still echo in my mind, "Do not judge people, Anne. God created us all equal and in His image."

While studying to be a teacher at Potchefstroom University, I was a finalist for Rag Queen and for the first time in my idyllic life was confronted by jealousy, betrayal and heartbreak – an experience which could have brought me to my knees. Not being street smart, all I had to fall back on were my mother's words of wisdom "Never leave home without looking your best; comb your hair, put on a pretty dress, wear lipstick, and your world will always look better!" Often, while crying on the inside that's exactly what I did – and survived.

The ah-ha moment!

My passion for empowering women was born by teaching them to make the best of themselves. "If you look good on the outside, you will feel better on the inside and can cope no matter what! That's not all. Empowering yourself is also about improving skills and changing the way you think." I did exactly that without really making a conscious effort to plot my course.

I met a fine young man who was a pharmacist. After my graduation, we were married and relocated to the popular seaside city of Durban, South Africa, where my husband bought a pharmacy business. I managed the front of the store, including the cosmetic counter. My abiding interest in the beauty and image industry was born. I qualified as a make-up artist and beauty therapist, and was the first person in South Africa to be trained and qualified as a color and image consultant.

My teaching wasn't forgotten. Occasionally I'd do substitute teaching (known in South Africa as "locums") thus improving my training and speaking skills. Never did I imagine what God was planning nor that I was about to reach another milestone in my journey.

Beauty and Colourworks

At thirty, our first beautiful daughter was born. My husband's business was flourishing and I started my own business, working from a small home studio. My business took off rapidly and as the women learned how to make the best of themselves, I was changing their lives. This inspired me to pursue my new career with even greater passion! My business outgrew my home and South Africa's first total make-over salon, *Beauty and Colourworks*, was established in booming Umhlanga Rocks, which is a seaside resort town, near Durban.

Women came from all over the country to be 'made over' and my staff contingent grew to seventeen in a year! I was subsequently nominated Business Woman of the Year. This story is recorded in my book of memoirs, *Tea at the Oyster Box*.

God's plan was taking shape. I was invited by women's clubs, schools, and churches to speak about image and color coding and was asked to write for local newspapers and magazines. I personally did the makeup for the models on more than seventy front covers of our South African magazines.

Writing – another milestone in my journey

I needed to write training materials, especially for the International Image Consultants Training Academy which I own today. Out of this necessity, writing became a new challenge. Afrikaans is my first language. English, my second. With determination, spell check and a good editor, it has become one of my greatest strengths. Writing has empowered me to confidently share my knowledge and expertise, as well as publish, and grow my business.

My journey continues

My journey is not at an end. My passion and I have come a long way. I firmly believe events, experiences and all the skills that have empowered *me* were God's way of calling me to fulfill my destiny—**a passion to train and teach women to make the best of themselves.**

I have a master's degree and am a *Master in Image and Etiquette*, and have received among others, the Best Trainer Award for Asia from International Beauty & Image Consultants Association in Singapore! I also became the women's page writer of the *Umhlanga Globe*, which prepared me to become a journalist and eventually the author I am today.

My journey's lessons, I share with you

In order to pursue your passion, you have to know who you are, what makes you happy, and what makes you feel energized. It is important to realize that your fulfillment in life is dependent on your becoming and doing what you were born to be and do. Our minds are so often bombarded with negative energies and ideas, it is imperative to know that if you can change your thoughts...you can change your life. So be careful of the following pitfalls and hone in on the following suggestions:

Ignorance

Ignorance is the most destructive force this world knows, and has destroyed the potential of millions. Go beyond your limitations. Learn as much as you can. Build your confidence and authenticity.

Despair and disappointment

Your attitude is the paintbrush of your mind. Never give up on your dream. Libraries are full of stories of famous people who pursued their passion and made a success in spite of setbacks. Walt Disney, Jack Canfield and Mark Victor Hanson (the creators of *Chicken Soup for the Soul*), Mother Teresa ... the list is endless. Your name could also be added to this list!

Overcoming

Our lives on earth will never be free from pain and problems. It is in our overcoming these hurdles that we become the people we can be. The 'cameo of our lives' gets sculptured so that we can reach our destiny. This also was a lesson learned, when my second daughter was born mentally handicapped...She has been my greatest inspiration!

Quick fix

There are no recipes for instant fame and success. There simply aren't any! Often we think we have found a way, but only hard work and dedication pay off in the end. Never give up on your passion...the rewards of hard work are always earned.

Arrogance

Arrogance is the opposite of humility which is one of the most powerful character traits possessed by many great people. I believe in the kinship principles, where the client is king—the client being those in authority, your colleagues, and your subordinates. Treat every person you meet with respect; learn good manners and etiquette as they are vital life skills. Life will greatly reward those with these skills!

Deception

Don't be deceived; you have to take responsibility for your own life. Deception occurs when we blame others for our shortcomings and in-adequacies or we rely too heavily on others for direction and purpose.

Violating principles

If you are violating your value system to get what you want, you will never succeed. Be a person who keeps to principles and lives a life of integrity; it will pay off!

Ask yourself the following questions:
- What are your natural gifts and talents?
- What are your greatest strengths and weaknesses? (Make a note of the strengths you recognize and those others notice in you.)
- What do you enjoy doing?
- When are you happiest?
- Who are your role models? What are your reasons for choosing them and the characteristics you admire in them?

By asking these questions, you will begin the journey of honing your unique gifts, discovering your destiny, and fulfilling your dream and passion. These questions sure helped me.

Many of my weaknesses have turned into my greatest strengths. Once I acknowledged that my strengths included influencing and empowering others, I turned one of my greatest weaknesses into one of my biggest strengths today—writing.

Once you have recognized your gifts and talents, that will be when you discover *your* passion.

In following your passion and never giving up on your dream, you will discover the importance of being authentic; that is what draws people to you and makes you significant in your uniqueness. You are not a copy of someone else; you are uniquely and wonderfully made.

My life is not extraordinary. It is just that, by God's grace, I discovered my gifts and talents, and against all odds used them to pursue my passion. I am so grateful to God for giving me a specific purpose...from the gifts and talents, background, hurts, life's experiences, world travels, my children, husband...to where I live and who He sends on my life path. I am so looking forward to the rest of my life, and to discovering what more God has in store for me until He calls me home. I will continue teaching and training women from all over the Globe, how to be irresistible for the rest of their lives!

This can happen to *you*...

You can be ravishing at 20...

Charming at 40...or Irresistible for the rest of your life!

About The Author

 Anne Dreyer is a sought-after motivational speaker, author, and image coach who lives and teaches Coco Chanel's dictum. With her warm and stylish personality, Anne infects her audiences as she trains and inspires them from her personal life's experience as a successful businesswoman and entrepreneur. Nominated Business Woman of the Year 2008, Anne founded both Colourworks International, South Africa's first Makeover Salon, as well as the first Image Consultants Training Academy. She is the founder and foreign ambassador of APICSA, the Association of Professional Image Consultants in South Africa, and a professional member of the Professional Speakers Association of South Africa. Anne, master image consultant and etiquette expert, knows and believes that every person can blossom where they are planted and can be irresistible forever!

Anne Dreyer may be contacted via:
anne@annedreyer.com
www.annedreyer.com

Passion Expressed

GINETTE OSIER BEDSAUL

"ARTIST OF BEING ALIVE"

The most visible creators I know are those whose medium is life itself;
The ones who express the inexpressible without brush, hammer,
clay, or guitar.
They neither paint nor sculpt. Their medium is being.
Whatever their presence touches has increased life.
They see and don't have to draw. They are the artists of being alive.

~ J. Stone

I discovered this poem soon after I found my life's passion: teaching how to live fully and passionately. To learn how to become an artist of being alive, a way of living so that our lives reflect our true spirit, power, beauty, love, and purpose.

I am passionate about being alive and experiencing life's journey. I am particularly passionate about life potentiality...who we can become by living authentically and how that type of life commitment can heal and expand our lives.

What does it take to be aware, alive and living to one's full potential? For me, it means being a transformational life coach and teacher.

We often look up to people who lead brilliant, meaningful lives. Those people who have sparkling energy, who make purposeful contributions, and have a deep sense of profound richness and glory. They seem focused, golden, blessed, brave, and somehow insightful to the secret of a life well lived. These people are usually very passionate people. They have an energy about them, a sentience which takes them beyond the everyday vanilla existence into living a Technicolor life.

Passion is the ingredient that skyrockets us to feeling fully alive. Passion is a feeling, an aliveness which belongs to each of us and is ultimately a choice of a way to experience our lives. This feeling of passion can be experienced on many levels; we can experience passion physically, emotionally, mentally, and spiritually.

Experiencing passion is not limited to a few moments in your lifetime…the big mile-marker moments of life when you feel a surge of passion: the day you first fell in love; the day you signed the papers on your first home; or the day you first held your baby in your arms.

Those experiences are passionate moments, but passion is potentially far more than a brief experience in a lifetime. Passion is also a deep awareness and knowingness, a way to experience and approach all the days of your life.

Passion is the fuel, the thrust of being fully alive. We begin to see and feel through the eyes of passion as we experience our lives…all the aspects of our lives. We can learn how to love with passion, learn with passion, grow in passion, heal with passion, passionately forgive, be passionately sad, grieve with passion, live, and even die with passion.

To cultivate and hold this life perspective, we need to get a sense of what passion really is. Yes, it is a feeling, but is also a tool by which we can guide our lives. We must learn how to find and hold our passion.

Living in a state of passion is beyond words. We must feel passion to have passion. We must find what makes us passionate. The feeling gives us a foundation to begin to build upon. Each one of us has something that we love deeply, that moves us, inspires us, that we are passionate about. It's important to know how passion feels.

Once you have a sense of what you are passionate about, you can begin building a passion plan. This passion plan is essential. What is it that you love the most? What makes you happy and feel the most passionate? The key is to have a plan, and to practice it so the plan becomes a tool for your life.

Ultimately, this can help you learn how to live all aspects of your life through the eyes of passion. We use what we feel passionate about to stimulate the feeling of passion, like priming a pump. This allows us to look through the lens of passion in all aspects of our life experiences.

In fact, the more you live in passion, the more passion will grow and expand. On those days when I need to have a passion jump start, I use my passion plan to get back into a passionate perspective about myself and my life. The goal is to be able to live in the feeling of passion.

Becoming an artist of being alive means we passionately seek life. My dear friend, Hazel, who is ninety-one years-old this year, is a magnificent human being and one of the wisest people I know. Her passion is visible. Her blue eyes twinkle. She walks several miles a day and looks at least twenty years younger than her chronological age. She is so passionate she shines and strangers come to her on the street, in the supermarket, in a restaurant, anywhere and everywhere to ask what her secret is to life. They want to know her secret.

She loves life and is committed to learning something new every day. She speaks about how important it is to stay in the present moment, to love the moment, make the most of the moment and passionately experience every moment.

Hazel has experienced many things. She was raised by a Swiss immigrant father and American mother on a ranch in Montana. She was married to her childhood sweetheart for over sixty years, became the matriarch and hero of a large family, gave birth to four children, and is a grandmother and great grandmother many times over. She has mothered and raised many, many more, who call her Mom and Grandma; who share stories of how her love inspired and shaped their lives. She has traveled extensively, loves cooking, and a good adventure. She single-handedly researched and reunited her family in Switzerland, traveling and living there, meeting them, learning more about her heritage. You might look at these experiences and imagine with such a lovely life, it is easy for Hazel to be passionate.

Not so. She has also experienced loss. She suffered a teacher's abuse and experienced the school board choosing not to protect the children. Her beloved parents divorced when she was young. A sleighing accident broke her back and punctured her body. She is a breast cancer survivor. At the age of eighty-nine, she broke her shoulder and arm and was told it was inoperable. She passionately fought back against the odds to heal it back to functionality.

193

She has seen the world shift and change and lived through two world wars. Hazel has grieved the physical loss of her parents, her soul mate and husband, her siblings, family members, friends, and a child. She has been a witness to the passion of life and death.

All of her experiences have deepened her loving resolve of life. She continues to be totally passionate and lives life with a full embrace. This is why she sparkles and why people respond to her. She is an inspiration. It is moving to witness how her choice to live in passion has created such a rich and beautiful life. She is teaching us something very powerful. Hazel is an artist of being alive...and I am honored to say she is my mother.

I have often heard the saying, "Do what you love and everything else will follow." It's true; focusing on what we have passion for in our lives helps to keep us in passion. Passion is like an energetic magnet which attracts more of the same positive energy. Using our passion as our true north is a powerful guide to experiencing a life well-lived.

Let's take an inner journey. The following meditation is for you to read through and practice in a moment of solitude. Read it first and then close your eyes and visualize the experiences, the more you practice this, the easier it will become and the more passionate you'll feel.

Relax, get comfortable. Take a deep breath, inhale slowly and exhale, take another deep life giving breath and gently exhale. Take another deep breath and this time breathe right into your heart; feel yourself centering into your body and exhale. Feel your heart and allow yourself to begin to feel free... to be free to feel, to remember your passion. What is passion to you...what is it for you...what does it feel like inside of you? Just gently allow yourself to remember a time in your life when you felt passionately alive...you might get an image of yourself at that moment or you may feel yourself experiencing that moment again. Just allow this for yourself. What are you doing or experiencing or being in this memory of yourself? Take a moment and remember when you were a child. What did you love about your childhood? What games did you like to play? What were you most excited about? When you focus on a passionate memory of yourself, feel it. What is it about that moment that moves you so much? Relax and grow quiet, your heart will gently give you clarity on your passion. As you begin to remember and feel the stirrings of your passion, hold that feeling within you, just as you would hold something most precious to you. If you are still searching for that feeling within you...tune to what you love. Do you love to ski, run, dance, learn, create, write, solve a good puzzle, be with animals or in nature? Do you love music, traveling or simply playing? Take a moment and allow yourself to remember and to reach the passion inside of you. Breathe right into that feeling within you. Feel your passion grow. Bring that feeling right into you at this moment. Feel passion now. Feel passion and begin to view your life today through the eyes of passion. Get the sense of how you can cultivate passion within, how you can hold it and how it imbues you and your life with a momentum, an inspiration, a force of joy! Allow yourself to remember what it is to be inspired, let yourself dream of the life you now lead through the eyes of passion, visualize your experience and feel it in your body. Notice how it makes you feel. Feel that palpable enthusiasm beginning to build inside of you. Stay with this feeling and grow very clear on what sparks your passion. Allow the remembrance of this feeling to blossom within you and remember that you have the right to live passionately—it is your birthright.

After you experience this meditation, you will find yourself moving toward a place of peace and clarity. This is the simple beginning of your passion plan. Stay with this process until you are clear what sparks your passion. You will want this feeling and experience to grow into a tangible plan that will help you feel and live in passion.

I am a very practical person. When I originally started learning about building passion in myself, my plan really helped me find, stay, and thrive in this state of passion. I love music; it moves me and speaks to me. I particularly love very inspiring, passionate music that lifts and builds feelings of movement, joy, and passion.

A friend and I made what we called the "passion tape." (Yes, I did say tape; it was a long time ago). It was magnificent for this work as it was a collection of all the songs which made us feel passionate. You could call this the quintessential mixed-tape. Actually it was far beyond that. This collection of music was put together with the intention to move us into passion and keep us there. I listened to it, sang with it and danced to it so many times I eventually wore the tape out. This music became my passion plan. It worked. To this day, all I have to do is think about the "passion tape" and I get inspired and passionate. It still reminds me of the feeling of passion, how to claim it and apply it to my present moment.

This has been a very valuable tool for me. It is powerful to know where my passion lies and how to harness powerful energy inside of myself. I encourage you to develop a "passion plan" for yourself. This easy and practical tool will help you reconnect with and stay in your passion. I have used my passion plan throughout my life...especially when times are challenging. I make every effort to stay in passion because I want to stay on the correct course for my life. Becoming an artist of being alive means that I must embrace all the experiences of my life.

Living in passion does not look a certain way. A commitment to live in passion means experiencing life with a deep love. How important is the quest to view and live life through the eyes of passion? Living passionately allows us to create what we really want in our lives, like weaving a beautiful tapestry. It sets a tone inside of us, a frequency within us that is not only how we experience our world internally, but also how we consciously create passion in our external world.

This is powerful because you manifest from who you are, not what you do. This sets an energetic tone which literally sends out wavelengths of energy. Each one of us is a transmission tower sending out energy and intention.

We begin to see and feel how powerful and on-course our lives are when we are living in passion. We can send a pure transmission of who we really are in a profoundly loving, powerful, and passionate frequency. This is how we become artists of our lives, how we create a truly authentic, passionate life. This is the moment when we become passion expressed.

About the Author

Ginette Osier Bedsaul has held leadership, training, and coaching positions with an international non-profit organization, worked for several Fortune 500 companies, and successfully created and managed her own award-winning entrepreneurial business for the past two decades.

Ginette has been a senior faculty member and counselor with the Training in Power Academy for over a decade. She is a senior minister with the Power of Spirit Church. Her work focuses on wellness, healing, meditation, and assisting others to the path of self-awareness.

Her interests are in vibration and transpersonal psychology, spiritual transformation, life potentiality, and the feminine face of God. She holds a bachelor's degree from the University of Nevada, Las Vegas and is pursuing her master's degree in psychology.

Ginette presently lives in Las Vegas, Nevada in the richness of a three-generational household.

Ginette Osier Bedsaul may be contacted via:
Ginette@bedsauls.com

A Final Thought...

Life is full of possibilities. It is up to us to open our minds to what "can be" and then make the choice to pursue it passionately.

Passion is thought turned into performance...it's the energy that propels you to your destination. It is one of our most important traits. Like confidence, passion is something you create for yourself.

First, you must have a goal that you want to achieve. Passion implies that you believe in yourself enough to go after your goal. Passion tells the world you have a dream, you have courage and you see success in your future. When you are passionate, you are willing to grow daily and adjust your priorities to achieve your desires.

Go after what you want with passion. Success is as competitive as any sport. Don't sit back and wait for someone to discover you. Get out there and do something. You have as much ability as anyone else.

Life is a succession of choices. You have the ability to choose. Choose passion.

Life Choices Books

If you would like to order additional copies of *Life Choices: Pursuing Your Passion*, please visit our website at www.lifechoicesbook.com or call 702-896-2228. Discounts are available on quantity orders.

Speakers

Most of the authors in this book are available for speaking engagements. If you would like to have one of them make a presentation for your organization, you may contact him/her at the contact address given at the end of their chapters or contact Turning Point International at (702) 896-2228.

Your Story

If you are an author or have a burning desire to tell your story, we are interested in working with you.

We are looking for stories that enlighten, inspire, motivate or entertain. Each of our *Life Choices* books focuses on a specific topic or passion. *Life Choices* books contain well-written, original, non-fiction stories that include one or more of the following themes:

- Life lessons you have learned and the impact they've had on your life
- How you overcame an obstacle or met a life challenge
- How you or someone you know maintained a positive attitude in spite of life situations
- An experience of a synchronistic moment, a moment of "fate," or something awe-inspiring
- Random acts of kindness and the impact they had on your life

Contributing to an anthology such as this one is the fastest, easiest, and most affordable way to become published. Published authors are recognized as experts. This is a simple, easy way to quickly establish yourself as an expert and gain credibility.

Call (702) 896-2228 to find out about upcoming titles and how to submit your story for consideration.

Life Choices Authors
Other Products

BOOKS

Life Choices: Navigating Difficult Paths
ISBN 978-0-9825264-0-8
Ginette Osier Bedsaul: *An Enacted Miracle*
Anne Dreyer: *Class is a Choice*
Charlotte Foust: *Invisible*
Sandy Kastel: *Detours*
Judi Moreo: *The Choice That Changed My Life Forever*
Mary Monaghan: *New Beginnings*
Sandra Gore Nielsen: *A True Love Story*

Life Choices: Putting The Pieces Together
Ginette Osier Bedsaul: *Inexorable Love*
Charlotte Foust: *Broken Mirror*
Bea Goodwin: *Twelve Dollars*
Ann Parenti: *After Thoughts*
Anne Dreyer: *Fix It*
April Aimee Adams: *Welcome to Life*
Judi Moreo: *Not Me!*

April Aimee Adams
That Don't Make Ya Bad: A Memoir of Addiction
Rodnee Books, LLC
Las Vegas, NV
ISBN: 978-0-615-32555-2

Judi Moreo
You Are More Than Enough: Every Woman's Guide to Purpose, Passion and Power
Stephens Press, Las Vegas, NV
ISBN-10: 1932173722

Achievement Journal,
You Are More Than Enough
Stephens Press, Las Vegas, NV
ISBN-13: 9781932173659

Ordinary Women, Extraordinary Success
Career Press, Franklin Lakes, NJ
ISBN: 1-56414-701

Conquer the Brain Drain: 52 Creative Ways to Pump Up Productivity
National Press Publications,
Shawnee Mission, Kansas

ISBN: 1-55852-299-9
Ignite the Spark: 52 Creative Ways to Boost Productivity
Penguin Books, Johannesburg,
South Africa
ISBN: 0 14302433 7

"Shotsie Career Cat"
The Ultimate Cat Lover
HCI Books, Deerfield Beach, FL
ISBN-13:978-0-7573-0751-5

"I'll Send You A Rainbow"
The Ultimate Mom
HCI Books, Deerfield Beach, FL
ISBN-13: 9780757307966

"The Robin"
The Ultimate Bird Lover
HCI Books, Deerfield Beach, FL
ISBN-13:978-0-7573-14384

Anthony Spiniccia
The Wonders of Chi Kung: Relieving Stress and Unlocking Glowing Health and Vitality,
Third Edition [Paperback]
CreateSpace
Seattle, WA
ISBN-10: 1451568894
ISBN-13: 978-1451568899

Darren LaCroix
Masters of Success
Insight Publishing Company, Sevierville,
TN, USA
ISBN: 1-60013-010-0

Speakers EDGE
Soar with Eagles,
Rogers, AR
ISBN-13: 978-0-9814756-0-8

Laugh & Get Rich
Specific House Publishing,
Kissimmee, FL,
ISBN: 978-0-9674586-0-1

Get Paid to Speak By Next Week®
The Humor Institute, Inc.
Las Vegas, NV,
ISBN-10: 0-9819587-3-7
ISBN-13: 978-0-9819587-3-6

How Professional Presenters Can
Own The Stage
The Humor Institute, Inc.
Las Vegas, NV,
ISBN-13: 978-0-9790062-7-2
ISBN-10: 0-9790062-7-9

Get More Laughs By Next Week ™
The Humor Institute, Inc.
Las Vegas, NV, USA
ISBN: 978-0-9825063

Path to Powerful Presentations
The Humor Institute, Inc.
Las Vegas, NV
ISBN: 096693097-5

YouTube It!
The Humor Institute, Inc.
Las Vegas, NV
ISBN: 978-0-9790062-2-7

Ridgley Goldsborough
The Great Ones
John Wiley & Sons, Inc.
Hoboken, New Jersey
ISBN: 978-0-470-48594-1

Anne Dreyer
Darling I Have Nothing to Wear
Colourworks International
South Africa
ISBN: 9 780620 330558

Darling What Fork Do I Use?
Colourworks International
South Africa
ISBN: 9 780620 330559

Tea at the Oyster Box
Osborne Porter Literary Services
South Africa
ISBN: 97809810448992

Dallas Humble
Make It Happen
ISBN: 978-0-9830052-0-9

Young, Slim, Fit and Sexy
ISBN: 0-9745696-3-1

A Healthier You!
ISBN: 1-932863-63-X

Kevin Parsons
Ken Johnson & Roxi the Rocker
ISBN: 978-0-9795405-0-9

CDs

Sandy Kastel
This Time Around
Only In Las Vegas
Silk and Satin Records, LLC 2007

Indiana Rain
Silk and Satin Records, LLC 2010

Ann Parenti
As Promised
Forgotten Song Productions
4261407712

AUDIO PROGRAMS

Judi Moreo
You Are More Than Enough
Every Woman's Guide to Purpose,
Passion and Power
Soundtrax (12 CDs)

Life Choices Books

Messages of Courage, Hope and Possibility
from 26 Inspirational Authors

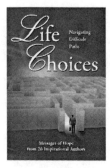

"Choices! We have choices. They are the source of the success in our lives. When things happen to us, we can choose to believe they happened for a reason. We can discover opportunities in the most difficult experiences if we are willing to look for them. It is what we choose to think about each experience that determines how we respond to it. How we respond determines whether or not we find richer, more purposeful, more joyful lives. We are the only ones who can choose our attitudes and the principles we live by. Choose well, my friends. Choose well..."

The **Life Choices** books are a series in which real people share their stories of overcoming obstacles, putting their lives together and following their passions to create successful, significant lives.

While the stories shared differ in context, they share a common thread of courage, hope and fulfillment. No matter what obstacles you encounter, or how many pieces your life is in, there is a way to find a new path, make a new choice and create a better life.

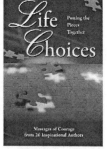

It is through life's challenges that we find our strength. It is the choices we make along the way that determine whether we remain victims of our circumstances or become victors. There is no such thing as life without struggle. No one comes out of struggle the same as he or she was when it began. Everyone has to make choices between giving up or growing stronger.

In the pages of these books, you will discover how the authors have taken a variety of paths to find their own way back to wholeness and success. May they be the inspiration for you to continue your journey, make new choices and create a new life.

www.lifechoicesbook.com

Is Writing Your Passion?
Do You Have A Story That Needs To Be Told or A Book That Wants To Be Written, but You Don't Know Where To Start?

Whether you are a beginning writer or a professional, a coach can be very beneficial to you. Coaching is a process, not something you can do for one session, take a test and be a pro. Coaches don't tell us what to do or how to do it. They give us suggestions and guide us. They provide alternatives for us. Most of all, there is an element of accountability. Are you on track with your goals? What's missing? What's needed? What's next?

It has never been more challenging to "succeed" than it is today. Whether in your personal life or writing a book, it is crucial to have skills, support and encouragement as you move toward the fulfillment of your potential. Judi Moreo's coaching provides thought-provoking approaches for overcoming challenges, unleashing your potential, and recharging your passion.

Judi is an internationally recognized speaker, author and coach who uses her more than 25 years of knowledge and experience to help others develop the skills and discipline necessary to achieve their personal goals.

Judi's nine books include *Conquer the Brain Drain, 52 Creative Ways to Pump Up Productivity, Ignite the Spark: 52 Creative Ways to Boost Productivity*, the award winning *You Are More Than Enough: Every Woman's Guide to Purpose, Passion and Power*, and the highly acclaimed *Achievement Journal*. As publisher of the *Life Choices* series, Judi has enabled first time authors to find their voices and assisted professionals in many fields to enhance their credibility by having published works.

She has successfully coached and mentored speakers, entertainers and first time authors through the process of writing and publishing their works. She has a unique ability to see possibilities in others and inspire them to reach their highest potential.

If you would like to speak with Judi about writing or publishing your book, call Turning Point International, (702) 896-2228.

to follow
your

CPSIA information can be obtained
at www.ICGtesting.com
Printed in the USA
FSOW02n1041220416
19563FS

9 780982 526439